Ripley's®

Big, Weird & DANGEROUS FISH

Written by:
Bob Cranston

with an Introduction by:
Joseph M. Choromanski

Original Art by:
Corena Ricks

Series Edited by:
Edward Meyer

SCHOLASTIC INC.

New York   Toronto   London   Auckland   Sydney
Mexico City   New Delhi   Hong Kong   Buenos Aires

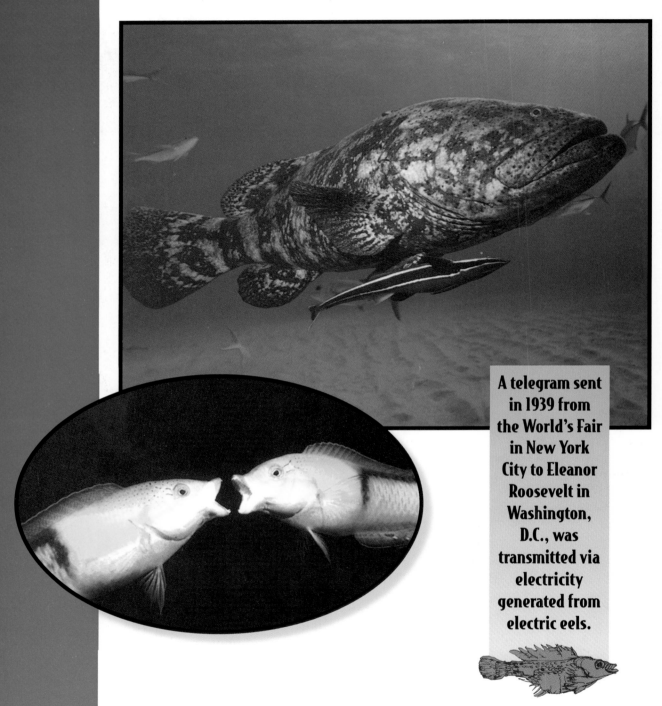

A telegram sent in 1939 from the World's Fair in New York City to Eleanor Roosevelt in Washington, D.C., was transmitted via electricity generated from electric eels.

Big, Weird & Dangerous was designed by Infinite Ideas & Designs, Casselberry, Florida.

ISBN 0-439-34274-0

10 9 8 7 6 5 4 3 2   1 2 3 4 5 6/0

Printed in the U.S.A.   1

First Scholastic printing, November 2001

Robert Ripley had a great interest in the creatures of the ocean, especially the odd and unusual specimens you will find in this book. He drew literally hundreds of fish Believe It or Not! cartoons during his lifetime, and he also collected specimens, both alive and preserved, for museum display purposes. In his house he had a large aquarium filled with fish that swam upside down and a species that shot water bubbles at its prey.

In his first odditorium in Chicago in 1933, he displayed three of the fish presented in this volume. The Crucifix fish, a strange catfish that has an uncanny resemblance to the image of Christ on the cross. The Diable de Mer, a scary looking creature that with a little human creativity takes on the appearance of the devil. The porcupine puffer fish, a fish that throughout time has been used both as a decorative item and as a weapon of war in various parts of the world. He was also the first person to unveil the Feejee Mermaid as the world's greatest hoax.

To create this book, the third in our ongoing Marine Life Series, we combed every fish cartoon we have ever published and chose to highlight just the biggest, the weirdest, and the most dangerous. The majority of the species featured are saltwater species, but a few freshwater fish have been included because of their special uniqueness. The piranha for example, is truly one of the most dangerous fish in existence (see page 46), and the sturgeon is certainly a *very big* fish (see page 9) despite its often being found hundreds of miles from the nearest ocean!

Many of the fish in this book are very rare, and not likely to be seen at pet stores or even aquariums. In some cases the species is known from only a handful of individual specimens, and in others, like the oarfish (page 53), scientists have actually learned more from studying the occasional dead specimen that has been found washed up on a beach, than they have from live specimens. Little is known about many of these exotic fish, and it is our hope that this book will ignite the interest of young readers to learn more about these mysterious creatures of the deep.

Bob Cranston, the author of this book, is a world famous underwater photographer currently living in San Diego, California. During his career he has filmed everything from the great whales to the smallest of crustaceans. Many of his award-winning photographs have been used throughout the book to illustrate his text.

We believe Robert Ripley would be proud of this latest book. Full of fun facts and unbelievable tales, it continues the Ripley tradition of providing entertainment while also providing the latest in scientific data. We hope you enjoy reading it as much as we enjoyed writing it. Enter now, the fascinating realm of Ripley's *Big, Weird & Dangerous Fish!*

Edward Meyer
Series Editor

Robert Ripley was the first person to expose P.T. Barnum's famous "Feejee Island Mermaid" as a clever hoax. He discovered it was nothing more than a fish tail sewn unto a monkey's head!

In 1940 Ripley broadcast the first-ever live underwater radio show. With the microphone inside his helmet, he described the awesome feeling of coming face to face with a giant seven foot long, five hundred pound Jewfish.

Introduction

Studying Marine Biology in a college in Ohio presented some interesting logistical problems, like no ocean. Consequently, I took summer courses at the Gulf Coast Research Laboratory in Mississippi. My first summer there I took Ichthyology (the study of fishes). As a part of this course we had to collect and preserve over 100 different species of marine fishes. I quickly discovered that an easy way to accomplish this goal was to hang out at the sorting line of the nearby catfood and dogfood factory. At the factory, large trawlers tied up daily to offload their catches of bottomfish. All of this catch was sucked out of the ships' holds by vacuum pump and was sent up to the factory via the sorting line conveyor belt. In this room, a dozen ladies stood picking out the more valuable shrimp to sell in the food markets. They also sorted out rocks, and other bottom debris that would not otherwise enhance the taste of the dogfood. It so happened that this conveyor belt was a great way for fish students, like me, to see and collect the greatest diversity of Gulf coast fishes. My first day on this line was amazing! I had never seen such a variety of weird looking fish! There were the long, silvery cutlassfish with their sharp pointed teeth and their deep-sea monster appearance. There were the pufferfish, some of which were still inflated with air like small balloons. There were gulf toadfish that tried to bite as they rode by. There were croaking croakers and winged sea robins, which to this day I still cannot distinguish between the twelve gulf species. There were stingrays and sharks of all size and description. There were even catfish and dogfish that ended up as catfood and dogfood. This fun experience no doubt contributed to my appreciation for the vast diversity of fish species and my continued interest in the most unusual, stranger species.

More recently, while working at the Monterey Bay Aquarium in California, I was fortunate to have worked on the collection and husbandry of the giant Ocean Sunfish (Mola mola), one of the biggest and weirdest fish in the world. Molas were collected as small juveniles, but they grew into giants very quickly. We collected one small 20 lb., 23½" mola in November and by the following September (287 days), it had grown to 56½" long and over 375 lbs.!!!

The Mola mola is just one of the many exotic, big, weird or dangerous fish you will encounter in this book, the third volume in Ripley's Marine Life Series.

Joseph M. Choromanski
Vice-President Husbandry
Ripley Aquariums, Inc.

Robert Ripley's Sunday color cartoon originally published July 7, 1946.

THE **FISH** THAT WALKS ON ITS TAIL !
SAILFISH FREQUENTLY STEP ALONG ON THEIR WRIGGLING TAILS AS MUCH AS *200* FEET

Contents

THE **GIANT SUNFISH**
WHICH WEIGHS MORE THAN A TON
GROWS FROM A TINY FISHLET —
NO LARGER THAN THE HEAD OF A PIN!

Big, Weird & DANGEROUS FISH

What Makes a Fish a Fish?

Fish are divided into 3 major groups:

- **Agnatha**– lampreys and hagfishes
- **Chondrichthyes**– sharks, skates and rays
- **Osteichthyes**– bony fishes.

The group **Agnathidas,** which means "without jaws" comprises a small group of primitive eel-like fishes, including lampreys and hagfishes. These are the most ancient of living fishes and generally inhabit very deep water. They have cartilaginous skeletons, and lack jaws or paired fins.

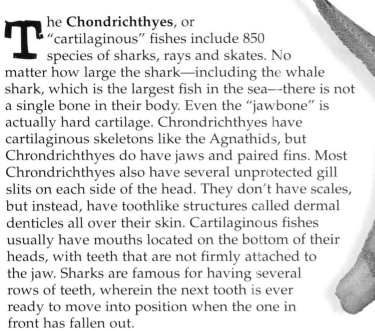

The **Chondrichthyes**, or "cartilaginous" fishes include 850 species of sharks, rays and skates. No matter how large the shark—including the whale shark, which is the largest fish in the sea—-there is not a single bone in their body. Even the "jawbone" is actually hard cartilage. Chrondrichthyes have cartilaginous skeletons like the Agnathids, but Chrondrichthyes do have jaws and paired fins. Most Chrondrichthyes also have several unprotected gill slits on each side of the head. They don't have scales, but instead, have toothlike structures called dermal denticles all over their skin. Cartilaginous fishes usually have mouths located on the bottom of their heads, with teeth that are not firmly attached to the jaw. Sharks are famous for having several rows of teeth, wherein the next tooth is ever ready to move into position when the one in front has fallen out.

The tails of cartilaginous fishes are not usually symmetrical, and their vertebrae extend into the upper part of the tail. These fish also have internal fertilization, and their young are usually born alive, although some lay egg cases.

Filefish are often found hanging around reefs in a nose-down vertical swimming position.

Fish never stop growing.

Uniquely shaped and camouflaged, the Harlequin ghost pipefish is hardly recognizable as a fish at all!

The appropriately named "crocodile fish" of Indonesia, has the same sinister look as its feared namesake, and is able to frighten predators away by its looks alone.

The seas near Norway are home to the brightly colored European dragonet. Wild colors and shapes on a fish can be part of camouflage, or warnings of poisonous spines, or attractions to potential mates, or just fantastic creations of nature!

The giant ocean sunfish which weighs more than 2 tons grows from a tiny fishlet no larger than the head of a pin!

To scientists, all bony fish belong in the classification **Osteichthyes**—which means Bony Fish in Latin. With more than 272,000 identified species in the world, the majority of fishes are in this category. Every fish in this category has a bony skeleton and breathes through gills. Most fish are exothermic, which means they control their body temperature by swimming into colder or warmer water. Most fish have scales, and an air bladder to control their own buoyancy. Most fish have a mouth at the front of the head, a symmetrical tail, and reproduce by spawning and laying eggs.

Caught off the island of Catalina, California, in 1910, this mola mola weighed over 3,500 pounds and for many years was the heaviest fish ever taken on rod and reel.

Some fish are loners, but others like these striped grunts, gather and move in large schools in order to dazzle and confuse predators.

Tiny juvenile fish often hide within the soft folds of jellyfish because larger fish cannot reach them without getting stung by the dangling tentacles.

This tomato grouper is not trying to eat the shrimp, rather the shrimp is providing a valuable service to the grouper by cleaning it of parasites.

Often called "the Missing Link," the strange chimaera has some body parts and characteristics of sharks, but other body parts are more like those of bony fish.

Chimaera produce two egg cases, which may take up to a year to hatch.

Ratfish or Chimaeras are sometimes called "The Missing Link" between bony fish and cartilaginous fish. Ratfish have a gill cover (operculum), weak bones that are pliable, no scales, and they lay eggs. The female Ratfish produces twin eggs, which hang from her body on long filaments. Embryos may remain in the egg cases for up to a year!

In this book we will focus on *Big, Weird & Dangerous Fish.* For information on Chondrichthyes fish, we recommend Ripley's *Amazing Sharks.*

The Really Big Fish

Tuna

Tuna grow up to 10 feet long and may weigh over 1500 pounds. They are amongst the fastest swimmers in the ocean, reaching speeds of 30 miles per hour. Tuna are streamlined for efficiency. For example, their eyes are covered by a transparent cover, which streamlines and protects the eye. Their pectoral fins fold back into special grooves, the head is rounded and smooth, and the tail is forked to reduce friction. Ridged scales behind the gills also help the fish to slip through the water at high speed. Tuna have a special way of breathing by which they can force water into their mouths as they move, so they don't have to gulp at water to get oxygen.

Tuna are able to swim constantly at a rate of 4 miles per hour without ever stopping—it is possible for a 15-year-old tuna to have traveled a half million miles. Yellowfin tuna can go from 0 – 45 mph in one second.

The Bluefin Tuna, which can weigh over 1,500 pounds, is so thickly muscled that it retains its body heat-making its body warmer than the water. Scientists call this "thermal inertia."

In all species of tuna, a spawning female releases approximately 100,000 eggs for every kilogram (2.2 pounds) of body weight. That means a 145 lb. (medium sized) tuna will release more than 6.5 million eggs in one spawn.

The longest straight-line distance known to have been covered by a fish is 5,800 miles, accomplished by a Bluefin Tuna. It was dart-tagged off Baja, Mexico in 1958, then was caught south of Tokyo, Japan in April 1963. During its five-year journey, the tuna's weight increased from 35 lbs. to 267 lbs.

June 6, 1999

Police: 10-pound tuna was weapon in assault

SAN DIEGO — A man was arrested on suspicion of assaulting his girlfriend in a supermarket parking lot with a 10-pound tuna, police said Wednesday. Nicholas Anthony Vitalich, 24, could be charged with assault with a deadly weapon, police said. He was arrested Tuesday. "People will use whatever weapon they have available. In this case it was a fish," said Lt. Jim Barker of the police domestic-violence unit. He added: "It's a serious incident." The man's girlfriend told police that she and Vitalich argued and that he struck her several times in the face and lower body with the 2-foot fish, which he had just bought. She suffered cuts and bruises.

THE MAIN ALTAR of the Church of Collioure, France, WAS CARVED BY JOSEPH SUNYER IN 3 YEARS FOR A FEE OF $600 - PLUS A TUNA FROM EVERY CATCH MADE IN THE AREA WHILE THE ALTAR WAS UNDER CONSTRUCTION SUNYER COMPLETED THE PROJECT A YEAR AHEAD OF SCHEDULE BECAUSE HE BECAME TIRED OF EATING TUNA (1698-1701)

Tuna are one of the fastest swimmers in the ocean. The Yellowfin tuna shown here can zip from zero to 45 miles per hour in one second, but still isn't fast enough to escape the nets of commercial fisherman.

Tarpon are super-predators that are hungry most of the time. Scattering baitfish like a silver tornado, they will gulp down as many as they can catch.

Tarpon

Tarpon are in a family of fishes that date back to the prehistoric Cretaceaous period. They are considered one of the most primitive of the bony fishes. Like many primitive fishes, tarpon are noted for their large individual scales, which can measure more than three inches in diameter. Tarpon have been seen to gulp air from the surface, and have strange, lung-like tissue in their swim bladders.

Tarpon are open-ocean broadcast spawners. This means the female, which produces as many as 12 million eggs in one spawn, releases her eggs into the broad ocean current, not near a reef or sheltered spot. The eggs can drift as far as 100 miles before hatching. The hatchlings look like tiny transparent ribbons, and do not resemble their parents at all. When the larval tarpon finds its way to shallow water and has reached about one inch in size, it suddenly shrinks. Then, in about one day, it further changes to abruptly take on the appearance of an adult tarpon, and then begins normal growth again.

Tarpon can reach 10 feet in length and weigh more than 350 pounds. With their stout bodies and large, upturned mouths, tarpon look like the serious predators they are. Although they can sometimes be encountered as solitary creatures, tarpon usually gather in schools ranging from 20 to 200 fish. Large schools of tarpon may inhabit a specific area or reef for years. Tarpon are not afraid of divers.

Tarpon can make spectacular jumps out of the water, and are a favorite big-game sports fish. They have been seen doing clear upward leaps of 8 to 10 feet out of the water and more than 20 feet in horizontal distance. Tarpon are not considered good eating, however, and most fishermen practice catch and release with this species.

Tarpon are capable of surviving in both fresh and salt water, a phenomenon most fish are incapable of. So while tarpon are usually considered a marine, coastal fish, they have been known to swim up rivers in Florida, Texas, and Mexico. There is even a freshwater population of tarpon living in Lake Nicaragua in Central America.

Tarpon have long upturned mouths and unusually large coarse scales.

Taken from fish captured in a special trap which targets spawning females, these cheese like sacs are the eggs of bluefin tuna. One medium-sized female tuna can release more than 6 million eggs in one spawning.

The One that Got Away: Harold LeMaster of Clearwater, Florida, fought a tarpon for 17½ hours, but then lost it!

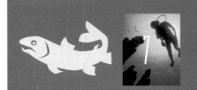

The Oblong sunfish is so rarely seen that when it appears in Honolulu Bay, Hawaiians reverently return it to the sea in the belief it is the ancestor god of all mackerels and bonitos.

Mola mola—The Ocean Sunfish

Molas appear to be all head, with no body or tail! They grow quite huge, up to 10 feet long and 5,000 pounds in weight, but when it hatches, a mola weighs only 4 ounces. A full-grown mola might well be the heaviest of all bony fish.

Molas show the greatest size difference in the fish world between the just-hatched young and a full grown adult. While adults can reach 13 feet across, a newly hatched mola is just one-tenth of an inch long. It is believed the eggs of the mola are released into the open ocean. Danish marine biologistJohannes Schmidt counted 300 million eggs found in one 4½-foot long female. A larger mola could probably carry even more!

The largest mola ever recorded was accidentally struck by a boat near Australia on September 18, 1908. *Wide World* magazine published this account on December 10, 1910:

> *. . . all hands were alarmed by a sudden shock, as though the steamer had struck a solid substance or wreckage . . . The boat's crew were astonished to find that a huge sun-fish had become securely fixed in the bracket of the port propeller. One blade was completely embedded in the creature's flesh, jamming the monster firmly against the sternpost of the vessel. It was impossible to extricate the fish at sea, so the . . . steamer proceeded on her passage to Sydney with the starboard engine only working. On reaching port . . . all hands were set to work to remove the fish. After much difficulty and with the aid of the steamer's winch, the sun-fish was hoisted clear and swung on board.*

The fish weighed 4,927 pounds and measured 10 feet in length and 14 feet from the tip of the top fin to the tip of the bottom fin.

Molas got their common name "Ocean Sunfish" because they appear to be sunning themselves when they loll around at the ocean's surface. They tip and turn, this way and that. When it is lazing around at the ocean surface, a mola can be mistaken for a whale or a shark. Whales and large sharks often have just the tip of their dorsal fin, which look the same as a mola's fin, sticking out of the ocean when they swim near the surface.

The Mola mola has the smallest brain, in relation to its size, of any vertebrate in the animal kingdom, and they have no tail. Their spinal cord is unusually short, too. In an 8-foot long mola, it was found that its spinal cord was only about one-half inch long!

They might appear to be awkward, but molas are actually good swimmers, and can even be remarkably quick when startled. Molas are found in tropical and temperate oceans, all over the world.

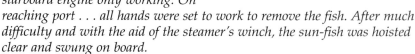

8

Groupers

This grouper is merely yawning. When eating, groupers can suck in their prey so quickly the human eye can not detect the opening and closing of their mouth.

Groupers are the best known members of the sea bass family. All members of this family, consisting of more than 375 species worldwide, have stout bodies and large mouths and lips. The larger species are generally solitary carnivores that lurk in the shadows of reefs, shipwrecks or kelp. Although ponderous in appearance, these chunky fish can cover short distances with sudden bursts of speed. They feed by suddenly opening their cavernous mouths, which creates a suction that pulls in their prey. Divers report they can hear a loud BANG when this happens. Divers see a fish in front of the grouper, hear a loud BANG, then notice the fish has disappeared from in front of the grouper—it all happens too fast for the human eye to see! The victims are swallowed whole. Groupers do not have sharp cutting teeth, or grinding teeth. A struggling fish is held inside the grouper's mouth with thousands of small, raspy teeth that cover the jaw, the roof of the mouth and the tongue.

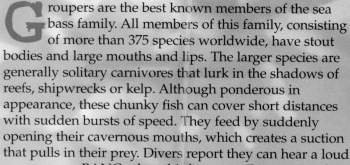

The Giant Sea Bass, also called the Jewfish, is the largest member of the grouper family. Once common in Florida, it is now rare due to spearfishing. It can reach 8 feet in length, and over 700 pounds in weight. The Jewfish can be bold, and has been known to charge divers.

Large, confident groupers sometimes allow close inspection by scuba divers, but are potentially dangerous and should not be approached. This giant grouper, or Jewfish, is being accompanied by a remora.

Sturgeons

In various European languages, sturgeon means "the stirrer," referring to the way these big fish move slowly over a muddy bottom, grubbing around for mollusks, worms and crustaceans.

The Russian beluga sturgeon is the largest species, reaching 28 feet in length and 3, 210 pounds. It produces the finest and most expensive caviar (eggs).

Sturgeon are weird looking, and hard to mistake for any other kind of fish. They have 5 rows of scutes (thick bony plates) that are arranged in definite rows. Sturgeons also have a protrusion like a nose, and dangling "whiskers" or barbels under their nose, just in front of their underslung mouth. They have primitive skeletons made up partly of cartilage and partly of bone. Their backbone curves upward into the top tail fin much like a shark's.

Sturgeons can live over 100 years, and depending on their location, they can grow from 14" to 25" in one year. They are bottom dwellers, and move back and forth from the ocean into the shallow parts of rivers, estuaries, and bays. They can often be found in "brackish" water where saltwater and freshwater mix.

In the 1880s and 1890s there were great sturgeon fisheries in California and Canada. Caviar was considered the food of kings, and the pricey sturgeon eggs created a booming and profitable business. Greed, waste and overfishing, however, nearly eliminated the Pacific Coast sturgeons. Reportedly the Canadian sturgeon fishery peaked in 1897 with a landing of more than a million pounds, but by 1901 a Fisheries Inspector declared the sturgeon "practically extinct commercially." In 1917 California banned all commercial sturgeon fishing, and now its sturgeon population has made a modest recovery. Where sturgeon of more than 20 feet in length were reported in the 1800s, a 10-foot long sturgeon is now considered huge.

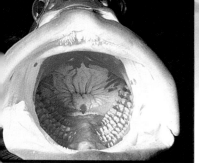

The longest sturgeon ever measured, a Russian beluga sturgeon, was an incredible 28' long!

The sturgeon has five distinct rows of armor-like scales called scutes. They also have chin whiskers, called barbels.

Sturgeon eggs are called caviar. Eaten as a delicacy, this salty rich food is quite expensive.

Billfish

The majestic billfishes are the most sought after of all the big-game fishes. They are the true fighting aristocrats of the sea.

There are two families of billfishes: The **Istiophoridae**, which are marlins and sailfishes, and the **Xiphiidae** which are swordfish. All billfishes have a sword or bill, which is a bony projection from the upper jaw. It is believed they use this as a club or "sword" to wound prey, or to threaten bigger predators.

Marlins

The Black marlin is not the heaviest fish of all bony fishes, but is certainly one of the biggest. Large specimens are documented to weigh in excess of 2,900 pounds and can reach lengths of over 20 feet.

Black marlins can be blue or black or slivery white. The Japanese name for a Black marlin is shirokajiki, meaning "white marlin." Marlin can also be striped. So how do you tell a Black marlin from a Blue marlin or a Striped marlin? One easy way to tell a Black marlin from all other marlins is that the Black marlin has rigid pectoral fins that stick out from its body, and cannot be folded back against the fish's sides like those of other marlins.

Large billfishes have a blood circulatory system that directs warm blood generated in the muscle core of the body around the brain. This keeps the brain at proper temperature and functioning efficiently.

Sailfish

Sailfish grow more than 10 feet in length, but are slimmer in build than other billfish and do not commonly weigh more than 200 pounds. A sailfish is unmistakable with its huge fan-like dorsal fin. It is a very fast swimmer, and has been clocked swimming at 68 miles per hour. A popular gamefish for its speed, fight and showiness, the sailfish is not good to eat.

When a sailfish is excited or feels threatened, it raises its sail. By turning to the side and raising the sail, this slender fish appears much larger.

Billfish can eject their stomachs out of their mouths and then swallow them again without harm! In this way they can expel foreign objects. It is not known whether this is done on purpose, or as a result of unusual circumstances, such as being hooked by fishermen. When a typical bottom-dwelling fish is hooked by a fisherman, and is quickly brought to the surface, the sudden expansion of the fish's gas-filled swim bladder pushes its internal organs out the fish's mouth. This is usually fatal for the fish, but for some reason, billfish don't seem to be seriously injured by their own weird version of "stomach turning."

Billfish are famous for their incredible high leaps straight out of the ocean. Caught in flight, this blue marlin was photographed off Kona, Hawaii.

Pelagic by nature, this striped marlin was photographed swimming more than 40 miles from the shores of Baja, Mexico.

Created by Californian artist, Larry Fuente, this Gamefish, a sailfish made from castaway board game pieces including mar jong and Scrabble tiles, hangs in the Renwick Gallery of the Smithsonian Institute in Washington D.C.

At birth sailfish are less than three inches long, and will fit in the palm of a small child s hand.

Swordfish

The swordfish, also called the broadbill swordfish, is one of the strongest and most aggressive of fishes.

Swordfish appear to migrate, moving toward cooler water in summer months and warmer water in winter. They are usually solitary fish, but occasionally are seen in pairs. The behavior of swordfish has been monitored off the tip of Baja California using sonic tags, which allowed a tagged swordfish to be followed for days at a time. Scientists found that the swordfish usually swam around a deep underwater bank at 300 feet during the day, then as the sun began to set, the swordfish would swim out further from shore and up near the surface of the ocean. At daybreak, the swordfish would return to its favorite bank near shore. Scientists speculate that the swordfish were feeding on bottom-fish on the bank during the day, and moving out to open ocean where squid rise up at night, to feast on tasty squid.

Swordfish are one of the most valuable of fishes, pursued worldwide by sport and commercial fishermen. In addition to its magnificent fighting skills, it is one of the finest food fishes, commanding very high prices in the world fish markets. Its aggressiveness is legendary, and many a boat captain has limped home with gaping holes in the side of his boat after a hooked swordfish punched it repeatedly with its massive beak. One skipper actually broke his ankle after a struggle with a swordfish that charged his boat fourteen times!

Billfish are believed to use their swordlike beaks to stun smaller fish before swallowing them whole. Pieces of swordfish bills have been found stuck in Blue and Fin whales—and other swordfish!

The research submersible ALVIN was rammed by a broadbill swordfish on July 6, 1967, at a depth of about 2,000 feet. The bill of the fish was stuck in a joint in the outer hull, and the fish had to be cut free when the sub returned to the surface.

Swordfish are one of the world's most sough after game fish, and are so aggressive, they will stab boats, whales, other swordfish, and even humans.

A 200-lb. swordfish rammed and sank a 90 ft. fishing boat off the coast of Valletta, Malta.

This squid fisherman from Vietnam was stabbed in the forehead by a swordfish! The fish's two-foot long sword entered through the man's forehead and exited at his right cervical spine. The man suffered temporary blurred vision, but no internal injuries, and returned to fishing within two weeks of the freak accident.

THE SWORDFISH WHICH FEEDS ON OTHER FISH—SUCH AS BLUEFISH, BONITOES, MACKEREL, ETC. HAS *NO* TEETH*!*

11

The WEirdoES

The Black sea dragon is a creature of the deepest, darkest depths of the ocean that dangles a lighted lure in front of its open mouth, hoping to tempt its next meal to within striking distance.

Deep Mysteries

The bathysphere, a round deep-sea submersible invented to explore the ocean's depths, was first used by William Beebe in 1930. It was a hollow steel sphere with one small, 15-inch quartz viewing window. The bathysphere was lowered as deep as 915 meters, dangling on the end of a cable. From this unusual underwater vessel Beebe observed many strange deep-sea animals for the first time.

The deepest swimming fish in the sea discovered to date is **Bassogigas.** One of these fish was recovered from more than 23,400 feet below the ocean's surface in the Puerto Rico Trench by Dr. Gilbert Voss.

Deep-sea fishes are exposed to a danger that comes to no other animal—the danger of falling up! Rapid ascent can cause air bladders to distend, and those fish that have gas-filled bladders will die in shallow water. This is one reason why deep-sea fish often do not survive the trip to the surface when they are caught.

The Black sea dragon has luminous teeth.

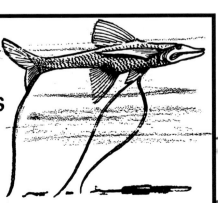

THE FISH THAT WALK — THE BENTHOSAURUS TRAVELS ALONG THE BOTTOM OF THE MEDITERRANEAN SEA *BY HOPPING ON 3 APPENDAGES*

The blind *Benthosaurus* probes for food on the bottom of the ocean with long extensions on its fins. It has no eyes, but can identify objects with its special, elongated, sensitive fins. Benthosaurus got the nickname "The Tripod fish," because it can stand on the ocean floor by propping itself up on long filaments that extend from its tail and pelvic fins.

The *Searsiidae* or **Tube-Shouldered fish** has the remarkable ability to emit luminous clouds out of small tubes located behind their pectoral fins. It is believed that they use this "smoke screen" for quick get-aways.

Pachystomias, a black dragonfish, emits red light from a light organ under its eye. Since most fish in very deep water cannot see red light, Pachystomias is able to use this light as a kind of invisible laser beam to hone in on prey then move in for the kill.

Bassogigas, a 5½ inch fish, can survive at a depth of 23,400 feet—yet a 3,200 ton nuclear submarine would be crushed in a dive to this depth.

The Benthosaurus, or tripod fish, has special, elongated filaments that extend from its body and are used by these blind deep-sea fish as feelers to find food on the bottom of the ocean.

The Weirdoes

The Deep sea swallower has a huge, hinged mouth that swings wide open to suck in its victims.

This Black swallower has a large meal in its stomach. Its stomach is extremely elastic, and its heart and innards can actually be pushed aside to make room for captured food.

Sea moths are named for their wing-like pectoral fins. They have unusual armored bodies and live their whole lives on the sea floor.

The **Chiasmodon niger,** or **Black Swallower,** can actually swallow a fish larger than itself. When this deep-sea hunter gulps up a victim, its heart and gills are pushed aside, and its stomach stretches enormously. To make a meal of this uncomfortable package, it carries the captured food doubled up in its stomach until it has been digested.

The deep-sea *Ultimostomias mirabilis,* a small 2-inch long fish, grows a single chin whisker 10 times longer than its body.

Malacosteus indicus is known as **Loosejaws,** because its lower jaw lacks a "floor" or bottom, so the mouth looks like it just has a floppy jawbone and teeth.

Labichthys elongatus is a deep-sea snipe eel. The males have very long and thin upper and lower jaws that curve away from each other. They feed by catching the long antennae of deep-water shrimps and tangling them in their jaws to attract prey.

Goosefish are notoriously aggressive predators, and they snap up all sorts of prey with their huge wide mouths.

The female deep-sea *Neoceratias spinifer* has long movable teeth that are fixed outside her jaws.

Goosefish have been found at depths of more than 2,000 feet. They are reported to be voracious eaters, with a tremendous variety of foods found in their stomachs—including sea birds and parts of sea turtles!

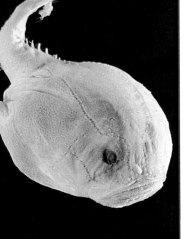

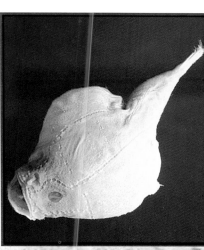

Photographed in a laboratory, after death, this is a pair of exotic toadfish. It is difficult for scientists to study these rare and hard to reach deep-sea fish in their natural habitat, and specimens seldom survive being brought to the surface.

Walking along on its special, spindly "fingers," this Spiny devilfish is making a dramatic display of its flashy pectoral fins in order to scare off predators. The Devilfish of Africa is so terrifying in appearance that parents use it to frighten disobedient children!

15

Luminous Fishes

When living creatures give off their own light, it is called bioluminescence. Scientists say bioluminescence happens when chemical energy is changed into light energy with very little heat being released.

Most marine animals that produce light make it in the blue or blue-green part of the color spectrum.

Gigantactis swims at a depth of 6,000 feet and lights its way through the ocean by a bright light that it carries at the end of a rod projecting from its head.

The **Deep-Sea Viperfish, *Chauliodus,*** has a row of lights along the outline of its mouth. Scientists think these lights can lure prey right into the jaws of the Viper. The Viper is well equipped with deep sea lighting, having many small lights in rows along the body, on its gill covers, and one large light right below each eye.

Hatchetfish have fixed eyes that can only gaze upward. They also have light organs along their bellies, so they will match the intensity or darkness of the water around them. In this way they hope to avoid making a silhouette which would attract the notice of any predator below them, looking up for a meal. The Hatchetfish, meanwhile, is doing the same thing, with its eyes forever looking upward for the silhouette of its next meal.

The sly Deep-sea viperfish uses bioluminescent lights around the edge of its mouth to lure fish into its deadly jaws.

The hatchetfish's eyes are permanently looking upward for the silhouette of prey. Meanwhile, the reflective plates around its own body reflect the color and light of the sea around it to avoid making an outlined target for other predators.

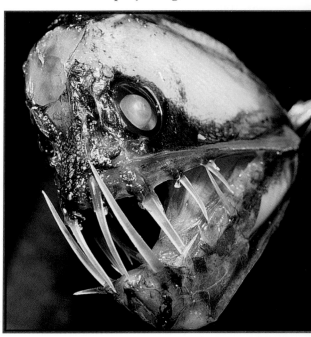

THE CHAULIODUS, OR DEEP-SEA VIPER FISH, HAS OVER 300 "LIGHTS" INSIDE ITS MOUTH *WHICH IT USES TO ATTRACT OTHER FISH!*

The Lantern fish has no eyes, but lights its way with a phosphorescent head.

Fish with Running Lights!

Photostomias guerni is equipped with two rows of phosphorescent spots that shine as it makes its way through the darkest parts of the ocean.

Grammatostomias, a deep-sea dragon fish found off Ireland, has several rows of luminous "portholes" and antenna six feet as long.

The sparkling sardine, *Scopelopsis,* lives in the dee[p] and exudes light through tiny "portholes" all over its b[ody]. The correct name for these "portholes' is photopores. Photopores are organs in the fish's skin that contain luminescent bacteria and have a transparent "window."

Banda Islanders of Indonesia use the luminous organ of *Photoblepharon* as bait because it continues to shine even after its removal from the fish!

In the 1970s, scientists diving at HydroLab, the United States' undersea habitat in the Caribbean Virgin Islands, saw many bright, moving lights around a coral wall near their lab. They only saw the lights on very dark nights. After some investigation, they discovered it was a new family of fish, which they called **lanterneyes**-after the light-emitting organ under each of the fishes' eyes. They produce this light, which they use for communication, and offense and defense, by means of luminous bacteria that live in a pouch beneath their eyes. These fish stay very deep or hide in caves during the day, but come up into shallows to feed on plankton on dark nights. The scientists further discovered that these special fish have their own ways of shutting off their unique lights. One kind of lanterneye, *Kryptophanaron,* shuts off its light by pulling a dark piece of skin over the light organ; it's a kind of dark eyelid that comes up from the bottom of the eye area. Other kinds of lanterneyes, *Anomalops* and *Photoblepharon,* have their lights mounted on long stalks and they can fit the bright end piece into a socket and, therefore, turn it to block out the light.

The Weirdoes

The special light organ under the eye of a lanterneye fish is a translucent patch of skin containing luminous bacteria. When a living organism creates its own light without heat, it is called "bioluminescence."

During the 1967 Arab-Israeli conflict an entire school of luminescent lanterneye fish was dynamited after being mistaken for enemy frogmen!

This school of lanterneye fish are swimming at a depth of 30 meters. The light organ under each eye shines out clearly in the darkness.

17

The Weirdoes

Deep sea angler fish lure food within range of their large gaping jaws by a light that grows from an antennae on their heads.

Deep Sea Angler Fish: Looking for Love

The bottom of the ocean is so dark and wide it is difficult for creatures that live there to find a mate.

The Deep-sea anglerfish is one fish that has difficulty finding a mate. Deep-sea anglerfish are considered extremely rare—scientist report catching an average of only one anglerfish in two weeks of scooping the sea trying to find one, and estimate that there are fifteen or more males for every female anglerfish. So the male anglerfish, which is very small compared to the adult female, has only one goal in life—to find a female and stay with her.

The female anglerfish has a luminescent light organ that shines out in the inky depths that probably helps the hopeful males find her. When a male finds a female, he physically attaches himself to her by biting into her side. He never lets go, and actually becomes part of her. His mouth fuses to her body, and blood vessels even grow between the pair. The male becomes a kind of parasite on the side of the female, but he also becomes a permanently attached sperm sac. Males will not mature until they are attached to a female, and females do not produce eggs that can be fertilized until they sense the presence of a male.

There are several species of deep-sea angler fish that have parasitic males. There is no fixed numbers of males that can be attached to a female. A female may have none, or as many as five males have been found attached to a popular mate. Each male is permanently attached for his entire lifetime. Depending on the female, and the status of her attached male, the "blushing bride" might be ten or twenty times larger than her mate.

Photographed in a laboratory, after it died, the bladder of this deep sea angler fish burst as it was raised out of the water, exploding out of its stomach into its mouth.

DEEPSEA ANGLER
(LINOPHRYNE ARBORIFER)
IS ALL HEAD, MOUTH AND TEETH WITH ILLUMINATED WHISKERS AND A LIGHT BULB FOR A NOSE
IT CAN SWALLOW A FISH 3 TIMES ITS OWN LENGTH AND NEARLY 10 TIMES ITS WEIGHT

The teeny male deep-sea anglerfish attached on the bottom part of the female s body, near the tail, has bitten into her skin, and eventually will fuse into her, until blood vessels grow between them.

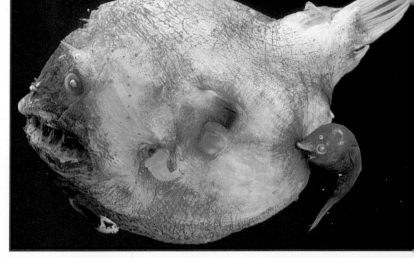

This gracefully curved seahorse has wrapped its strong tail around a bit of coral to prevent being swept away with the ocean's currents.

Seahorses

What has the head of a horse, the tail of a monkey, and the pouch of a kangaroo? And it breathes water? The seahorse, of course.

The seahorse is considered the slowest fish. Their swimming ability is limited by their rigid body structure, and their major source of propulsion is the wave motion of the weak dorsal fin on their backs. This makes a ripple and sends the seahorse forward in an erect posture. Seahorses are incapable of swimming against the current, and to avoid being swept away, they hang on to sea grass and coral strands with their monkey-like tails.

Seahorses spend most of their time gripping onto something, a bit of sea grass or soft coral, and waiting for the sea current to bring them something to eat. Their face is shaped like a straw, which is perfect for slurping up tiny food, like mysid shrimps.

This Pygmy gorgonian seahorse is cleverly camouflaged to look like bright red soft coral with puffy polyps. Seahorses are not built for speed and instead of trying to out swim their predators, they must rely on going unnoticed.

The Weirdoes

This longsnout seahorse lives in the warm ocean waters around Florida, and has no strong swimming fins. Seahorses live virtually their whole lives holding onto something, and waiting for food to come to them.

There are about 32 recognized species of true seahorses. Male seahorses are famous for taking on the duty of giving birth. The female seahorse passes her eggs to the male, and then he carries them in a pouch on his body. Devoted male seahorses have been known to give birth to as many at 142 new seahorses in a single batch!

Seahorses, which are rich in iodine, were used by the Chinese as early as 770 BC to treat thyroid problems. In ancient Japan, they were worshipped as "dragon's children."

Swollen with growing baby seahorses, this Pacific seahorse—one of the largest species of seahorse—is a very pregnant male!

Seahorses contain large amounts of iodine and dried seahorses used for medicinal purposes, sell for up to $90 an ounce in the Orient.

There is an especially extravagant kind of seahorse living in the waters off Australia that has evolved to look just like seaweed. It is called the Leafy Sea Dragon. Its long appendages trail in the water and wave in the current just like kelp leaves. Its coloration is a perfect match too. This kind of camouflage is important for a fish with an awkward shape that is not exactly streamlined for speed swimming.

海　　馬
10g　3500円

Wonderfully suited for drifting among the sea weeds near Australia, the Leafy Sea Dragon's special shape and coloring camouflage it perfectly in its environment.

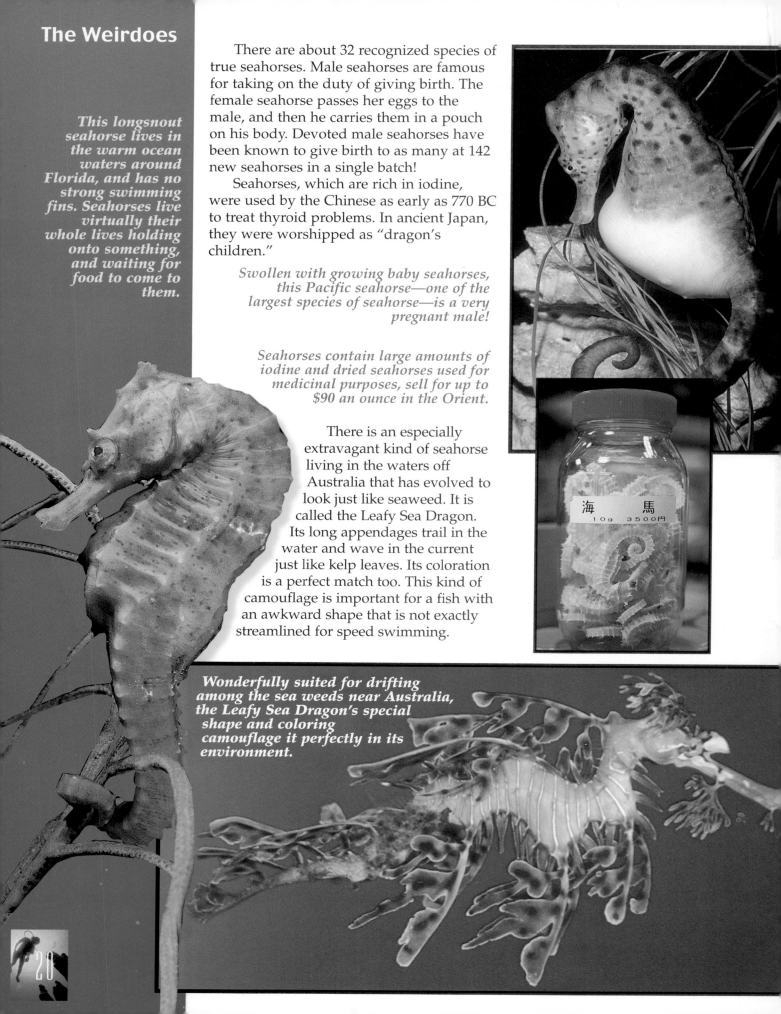

STYLEPHORUS
A DEEP-
SEA FISH
WITH A TAIL
FIN TWICE AS
LONG AS ITS
BODY, ALWAYS
SWIMS
VERTICALLY

Vertical Swimmers

There are other fishes in the sea, besides seahorses, which are comfortable swimming on either their heads or tails.

The pygmy filefish tries to hide from its enemies by swimming in a head-down position near soft corals.

The standing fish of the Sargasso Sea, *Stenarchus albifrons*, can remain standing on its tail for hours.

Shrimpfish in the warm seas around Papua, New Guinea, are commonly seen swimming nose-down. They feed primarily on minute crustaceans and are popular aquarium pets. In the wild they are seen in large schools, shimmering in the light and swirling over spiky staghorn coral. This fantastic display probably dazzles and confuses potential predators.

The filefish escapes enemies by standing on its head and imitating eel grass.

Imagine the sight of a whole school of shrimpfish hanging head down over a reef—a mesmerizing scene to behold, and probably very confusing to predators.

These scrawled filefish are eating a jellyfish. Filefish are quite comfortable in the head-down position, and often hide in reef structures with their noses straight down.

This tiny, baby filefish would be a tender morsel for any hungry sea hunter, so the little fish joins with a leaf floating by, hoping it will look like part of the stem in order to elude predators.

The Weirdoes

Species of trunkfishes that grow pointy horns are called "cowfishes"—for obvious reasons!

The trunkfish, an odd shaped three-sided fish, shoots water bombs at its prey and often looks like it is puckering up for a kiss.

When a trumpet fish gets nervous, it will stand on its head in a batch of soft coral and try to blend in.

An itchy Creole wrasse begs to be cleaned by a blue and yellow hogfish. There is another wrasse just behind the first, also turned nose-down, saying, "Me next!"

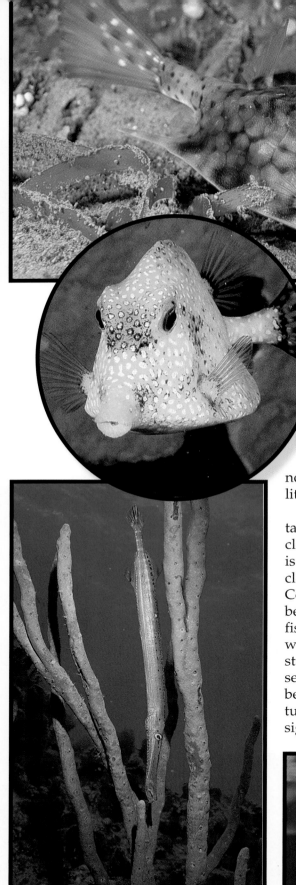

The trunkfish is a charming, small reef fish that looks like it is always puckered up waiting for a kiss. The special shape of its mouth makes a perfect cannon for shooting little blasts of water, which it uses to dislodge small worms and other bits of food from the reef.

Trunkfish are often seen turned nose-down along reefs, blasting up little puffs of debris.

Many fish stand on their heads or tails when they are lining up for a cleaning. A popular service in the sea is the grooming service that little cleaner fish provide to bigger fish. Certain spots on the reef are known to be "cleaning stations" where cleaner fish wait for "customers." Fish that want to be cleaned go to the "cleaning station." Cleaning is such a popular service, fish actually line up waiting to be cleaned. Fish at the head of the line turn nose down, or tail down, to signal: "My turn, please! Me next!"

Changing Body Parts

It might seem incredible, but there are some fish that begin life as females, but later change themselves into males! Scientists studying this surprising phenomenon call it sequential hermaphroditism.

Scientists now say that entire groups of fish are sequential hermaphrodites. For example, all groupers begin their lives as females. The groupers that are successful and survive to maturity eventually produce eggs, and then, amazing as it seems, they change their gender and become functioning males.

Female Sheepshead become males at about eight years of age. They lose their subtle pinkish color and slender faces, and take on the male form with vivid harlequin coloring of black, red and white. They also grow a steep forehead, projecting brow, and big, threatening teeth.

All anemonefishes change from being male to female. This is especially unusual because other fish that change gender start out as females, then change to males.

Rascally Wrasses

It has been found that most wrasses—maybe even all of them—have the ability to change their gender! In a gathering of wrasses, you will find three kinds of males: the supermale who is fertilizing all the eggs, primary males, who live their entire lives as males and hope to become a breeding supermale someday, and secondary males who began life as females then lived long enough to change into males. The dominant supermale can be spotted by his special, flashy color. He dominates a territory on the reef and controls spawning with all the females inside his territory. The primary males are more plainly colored-like females-and are left sneaking around and trying to spawn when there are large gatherings of females. If for some reason the dominant supermale is removed, or dies, the next largest and most dominant male or female will become the new, dominant supermale within a few days.

The beautifully colored Sunset wrasse (above), and the male Cuckoo wrasse (below) are "supermales" advertising that they are in charge of fertilization and looking for mates.

The female sheepshead has red-pink coloration and a slender build.

The male sheepshead is black-red-white and heavier built. This male sheepshead, when it was younger, was a red colored female.

23

The Weirdoes

The California kelp forest is home to many species of fish that spend their entire lives hiding amongst the ever-waving leaves.

The clever kelpfish is able to quickly change its color to match the surrounding kelp, then it imitates the waving motion of a leaf.

The male cabezon will not abandon his post guarding the greenish mass of eggs that he has fertilized. Fortunately cabezon are masters of disguise and can match the color of the reef around them for camouflage.

The Caledonian stinger buries itself in the sand then waits for food to swim by.

Masters of Disguise

The Kelpfish might look unremarkable when it is swimming casually around a California kelp forest, but if it needs to hide from an approaching fish, the Kelpfish puts on its "leaf" disguise. It puts its nose up to a stalk of kelp, takes on the color and shade of the kelp, and lets its body wave in the current, just like the surrounding kelp leaves. The fish's color match can be quite good, even taking care to duplicate the white splotches which grow on kelp leaves. The Kelpfish is slender, with the same outline as a kelp leaf, complete with rippled edges. Predators swimming by will not even notice the tasty but clever kelpfish right there under their noses.

Each female Cabezon lays a clutch of 50,000 to 100,000 eggs. The male Cabezon must rely on very good camouflage to protect himself, as it is his duty to stand guard over the clutches of eggs he has fertilized. The eggs are laid in piles, exposed on the reef, so the male is also exposed as he sits over them. Cabezons have tufts of skin that look like algae, and they are also skillful at matching the color of the reef they sit upon. The male Cabezon is dedicated, and it is difficult to scare him away from his position. The Cabezon is a big Pacific reef fish, growing to more than 3 feet in length.

This photo shows three batches of cabezon eggs in different stages of development. Each egg batch grows darker as they develop. You can just see the shining pairs of eyes of the cabezon larvae in the darkest eggs at the far right.

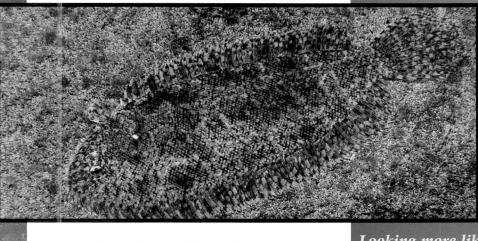

Flounders and flatfish are especially good at mimicking the color of the sea floor upon which they rest. In experiments, a flounder was even able to recreate a checkerboard pattern it was lying on! Scientists have discovered that only one of a flounder's eyes is able to sense the color of the area around it. If that one eye is covered the fish is unable to match the surrounding sea floor.

The Mediterranean Stargazer captures its prey by flicking its long red tongue, which looks so much like a wriggling worm that small fish come close to snap at it.

A popular trick used by many species of reef fish is the False Eye Spot. This defensive coloring is usually found on or near the tail of a fish. When a predator is zooming in for the kill, it typically will aim just ahead of the eye so the fleeing fish will move into the bite. If the prey fish can fool the hunter into aiming for the wrong "eye," the little fish can escape in the opposite direction!

Often fish with a false eye spot also have cryptic eye coloration. This refers to a disruptive color pattern, many times a dark stripe, that runs through the real eye. This is also designed to make it hard for a rapidly moving predator to distinguish which end of the prey to aim at.

Moorish Idols have several visual distractions at work. They often move around in schools, their unusual shape and coloration make it difficult to determine which end is the face, and their eyes are hidden in the middle of a series of lines.

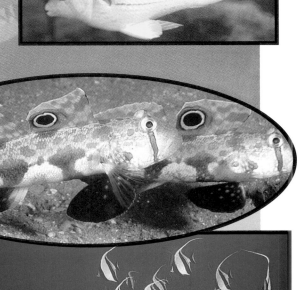

Looking more like a fossil imprint, than an alive healthy fish, this flatfish has done a super job of blending into the sea floor near Cocos Island, off Costa Rica.

Butterfly fish have a huge "false eye spot" near their tail, which is much more noticeable than their real eye!

These twinspot gobies have two big eye spots each, plus a dark stripe that runs through their real eyes. There are enough splotches and blotches here to confuse even the smartest predator.

Moorish idols don't have any false eye spots, but the dark stripes on their bodies effectively hide the round shape of their eyes. Their unusual shape and the way they move in synchronized schools, effectively make things difficult for their predators.

The Weirdoes

When it first hatched out of its egg, this flatfish was shaped like most other fish, with an eye on either side of its head. As it matured, its head shape changed and one eye "migrated" to the opposite side of the fish's face.

The eyes of the peacock flounder can rotate independent of each other, enabling the fish to see in two different directions at the same time.

The fine, long filaments trailing off the fins of juvenile pompano fish look very much like the stinging tentacles of drifting jellyfish.

Teenagers!

The juveniles of many fish species are so unlike their parents that scientists sometimes mistakenly put the juveniles in a classification of their own, only to later discover that they grow up into an already recognized species. Juvenile fish often have different, brighter, coloration than adults of the same species.

The young "hilly bodied" *Oreosoma* fish is so named because it appears to be covered with horns instead of scales. Actually, it does have very tiny scales and eventually "Oreo" grows out of its ugly juvenile "bumps."

Pancake-like flounders start life looking like regular fish. A few weeks after hatching, however, and just before settling to the bottom, the pelagic larval stage undergoes an amazing transformation. The skull twists and one eye migrates through a slit in the head and settles next to the other eye. The "top" side develops more pigment while the underside remains mostly white. The different species of flounder or flatfish are divided into left-eyed or right-eyed depending on which side of the body both eyes end up. Flounders' eyes are able to rotate 360 degrees, and each eye is able to turn and see independently of the other.

Juvenile pompano trail long silvery threads from their fins, which the adults do not have. It is believed that the juvenile fish are disguising themselves as venomous jellyfish—which also trail long filaments—to discourage predators.

Frogfish

Frogfish do not swim very well, and rely on looking like sponges. Frogfish have a lumpy texture, and will show the same color as a sponge they sit upon—even copying such details as little specs of algae sprinkled here and there, and small pores all over their bodies—all just like their favorite sponge!

Frogfish are named for their lumpy shape, and their special "hands." They have arm-shaped pectoral fins, including an "elbow" joint, and have the ability to grip the sponge they sit upon. Not shaped for swimming, they sort of waddle along instead, wriggling back and forth using their "arms and hands" to travel. Frogfish have one thing that real frogs probably wish they had—their own "fishing pole!"

Strategically placed just above the frogfish's mouth and in front of its eyes is an unusually formed first dorsal fin. The small protrusion extends outward, then ends in an intriguing little shape that the frogfish is able to jiggle—just like a fishing pole with a lure attached. The frogfish sits quietly on his sponge seat, trying hard to look like part of the sponge while he enticingly dangles his bait.

Researchers give the frogfish the prize for being the fastest eater! Using high-speed film work, and studying the action frame by frame, it has been found that a frogfish can open its mouth and engulf prey in less than 6 milliseconds. Other fish nearby are unaware anything has even happened.

There are about 60 species of frogfish worldwide. Frogfish are related to anglerfishes, goosefishes, handfishes, sea toads, many deep-sea fishes and the equally weird batfishes.

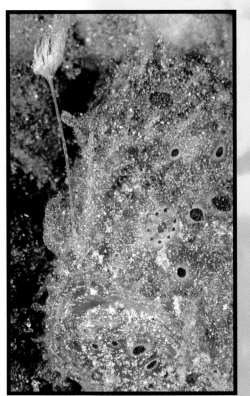

27

The Weirdoes

The peculiar fins of the batfish are better suited to walking on the ocean floor than swimming.

Batfish

There are about 70 species of batfish worldwide. Batfish are one of the most bizarre fish in the sea, and in many ways they don't look like fish at all. Instead of swimming, batfish use their pelvic fins to help them walk around on the bottom. In a panic, a batfish might try to swim, but the result of its effort is rather comical.

To capture food, batfish lie on the sea floor, and sometimes bury themselves in the sand. They stick the appendage on the edge of their face out in plain view, and hope a curious little fish will come close enough to investigate, so the batfish can then gulp it up.

A Galapagos Island batfish makes its stand on the sandy ocean bottom. Batfish spend most of their time buried in the sand, and are actually a rare treat for divers to find.

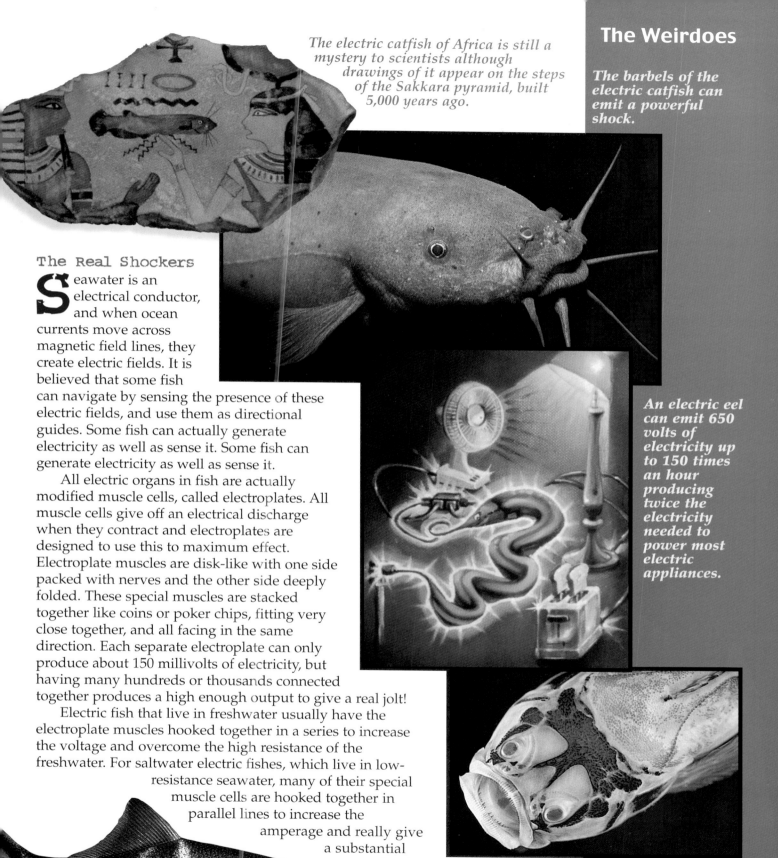

The electric catfish of Africa is still a mystery to scientists although drawings of it appear on the steps of the Sakkara pyramid, built 5,000 years ago.

The barbels of the electric catfish can emit a powerful shock.

The Real Shockers

Seawater is an electrical conductor, and when ocean currents move across magnetic field lines, they create electric fields. It is believed that some fish can navigate by sensing the presence of these electric fields, and use them as directional guides. Some fish can actually generate electricity as well as sense it. Some fish can generate electricity as well as sense it.

All electric organs in fish are actually modified muscle cells, called electroplates. All muscle cells give off an electrical discharge when they contract and electroplates are designed to use this to maximum effect. Electroplate muscles are disk-like with one side packed with nerves and the other side deeply folded. These special muscles are stacked together like coins or poker chips, fitting very close together, and all facing in the same direction. Each separate electroplate can only produce about 150 millivolts of electricity, but having many hundreds or thousands connected together produces a high enough output to give a real jolt!

Electric fish that live in freshwater usually have the electroplate muscles hooked together in a series to increase the voltage and overcome the high resistance of the freshwater. For saltwater electric fishes, which live in low-resistance seawater, many of their special muscle cells are hooked together in parallel lines to increase the amperage and really give a substantial shock.

An electric eel can emit 650 volts of electricity up to 150 times an hour producing twice the electricity needed to power most electric appliances.

The snout of the so-called elephant nose Morymyrid, is used to shock its prey with a strong electrical jolt.

The electric stargazer has eyes on the top of its head, and muscles behind its eyes that produce electricity!

29

The Weirdoes

The California flying fish cannot flap its wings; it sails through the air by gliding while holding its pectoral fins fully extended.

Up, Up and Away

Flying fish look like any other slender schooling fish, such as sardines or mackerel. If a hungry predator, however, gets too close to a flying fish, surprise! The fish sprouts wings and leaps out of the ocean, taking flight through the air, then landing into the water again some distance away. These agile fish are able to glide for hundreds of feet. Flying fish are a favorite food of marlin, and marlin will leave the water in pursuit of an escaping flying fish.

The Flying gurnard has enlarged pectoral fins that are colorful and beautiful, but they are not "wings." It was once believed that they could fly or glide out of the water like true flying fish, but in fact gurnards seldom leave the bottom at all, using their pelvic fins to walk along the sea bottom.

Gurnards look like they should be good gliders like their relatives the flying fish, but in fact prefer to strut across the ocean floor, often with their colorful wings extended in a dazzling display of color.

30

What's that Noise?

The so-called "Silent World" under the ocean's surface is not really silent at all.

Seahorses make little pops or snapping noises, when they are introduced into a new environment, or are experiencing a new situation. It is not clear what they are accomplishing with the noise.

Grunt fish got their name because they are able to make a grunting noise. Usually they do this if they are touched or otherwise disturbed.

In spring, along the coast of California, the males of a type of toadfish known as a midshipman advertise for females with a "beeoop" noise that sounds similar to a foghorn. To create the sound, the fish contracts and relaxes its swim bladder muscle at a rate of 200 times per second—more than twice the speed of a rattlesnake's rattle. This is the fastest muscular contraction measured in any vertebrate animal. The sound is loud, and carries long distances-it can even be heard out of the water. The "beeoop" calls can also be heard through boat hulls, and often disturb the sleep of people living on boats. Every spring these people make complaints about "secret Navy experiments" and other imagined causes of the annoying noise.

Groupers vibrate their air bladders to make a loud boom that warns other fish away from their territory.

Male bicolor damselfish make a single chirp before attacking an intruder, two chirps when readying themselves to spawn, three chirps to signal females that they are ready to mate, four or five chirps when a female approaches the nest but tries to leave without spawning, and other sounds while in their nest.

The Sea Robin (Prionotus carolinus) by vibrating its swim bladder makes noises that resemble a squeal or cackle.

The toadfish has a voice like a steamboat whistle.

The Weirdoes

Seahorses are able to make little popping noises if they are investigating a new place or situation.

The Jewfish, or giant grouper, warns other fish away from its home territory by making bellowing noises and swimming with its gaping mouth wide open.

This beautifully marked toadfish, found near Cozumel, Mexico, makes strange haunting noises at night.

The Weirdoes

Grunion risk their lives by leaving the ocean completely to spawn on sandy beaches under the light of the full moon.

Female grunion fish insert themselves, tail down, into wet sand. A male grunion then curls around her exposed upper part, and releases milt to fertilize the eggs she is depositing below.

Shore Leave

Grunions are small, slender fish found on the Pacific Coast from San Francisco to Mexico. When they are about one year old, and five inches long, they have reached maturity and are ready to spawn. This is when grunion do something amazing and weird-they leave the ocean completely and lay their eggs high and dry, up on sandy beaches.

In the spring and summer, three or four nights after a full moon, the grunion gather in the dark and wait for the nighttime high tide. An hour or so after the highest part of the tide, a female swollen with eggs risks herself by swimming out of the water as high up as she can go, onto the beach. If she finds that no brave males have accompanied her, she will try to wriggle back to the ocean. If she has some escorts, she wriggles with her tail and digs herself into the sand tail-first, straight up-and-down, so just her head is sticking out of the sand. Males curl around her exposed head, and fertilize the eggs she releases into the sand below.

An energetic female grunion will spawn from four to eight times each year laying from one thousand to three thousand eggs each time. The eggs incubate in warm sand, ideally between 61 and 81 degrees Fahrenheit, and will hatch in approximately 10 days, during the next lunar high tide. The maturing embryos require the agitation of the wave action to help them break out of the strong egg shells.

The fishing laws for grunion are unusual in that they require fishermen to use only their bare hands when capturing this slippery fish. Of course seabirds are allowed to use their beaks.

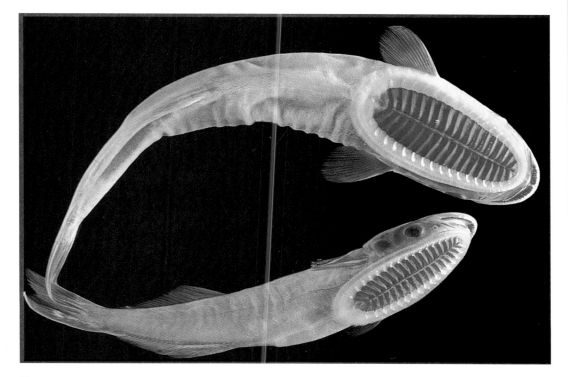

Remoras use plates on the tops of their heads to attach to sharks and other large fish. The suction action is quite strong, and can leave a painful bruise on a diver.

Tagging along for a free ride on a manta ray, this big remora is actually upside-down. Remoras appear to be as comfortable riding upside-down as right side up.

Remoras

The remora is a peculiar fish that spends its life riding on bigger fish, often upside down! It holds on with a suction cup on top of its head. This suction cup is actually a very specially modified dorsal fin. Although its common name is "Sharksucker," remoras attach themselves to different fishes, sea turtles and even human divers.

Remoras are quick and agile, and can move around their host even while both are moving rapidly through the water. The suction cup on a remora is strong enough that the remora can hang on, even while the host is moving quickly. Human divers have reported that remoras trying to attach to people can leave a painful bruise. Divers say that an unwanted remora is most easily detached by pushing the remora forward. The host animal carrying a remora may not like its uninvited guest, and maybe one reason why dolphins jump and spin out of the ocean is to remove pesky remoras.

Remoras are often found on baby Sperm whales, but not on adult whales. Adult Sperm whales dive to great depths to find the squid they eat, and perhaps remoras cannot stand the great pressure of deep water. Divers have reported seeing remoras on baby whales eating up leftover milk that the mother whale squirted into the water for its baby.

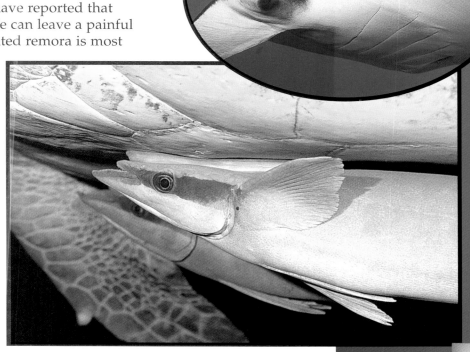

This pair of remoras, attached to the underside of a loggerhead turtle, are right side up, with the tops of their heads stuck onto the turtle's belly.

—Blue Meanies—
Dangerous *fish*

Big Caribbean barracuda patrol their turf like soldiers, often making divers nervous by following them around.

Barracuda

The Great Barracuda is impressive. It grows 6 feet long, has a large hooked jaw, and its thick teeth protrude menacingly from its mouth. It is common in Florida, the Bahamas and the Caribbean. This big, toothy fish has the unnerving habit of approaching divers and following humans around reefs. Barracuda are especially dangerous if there is bait in the water. Spear fishermen are occasionally attacked by hungry barracuda.

A barracuda s teeth are especially long and protruding, and are ideal for puncturing flesh.

Nadine Cloer of Key West, Florida, required 200 stitches to her hands and legs after an 8 ft. long barracuda leapt out of the water and attacked her!

The teeth along the sides of a barracuda's mouth look like a row of silver bullet heads.

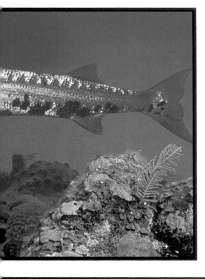

THE BARRACUDA

WHEN IT IS ASLEEP DISPLAYS DARK STRIPES ON ITS BODY—BUT IT CAN MAKE THEM DISAPPEAR WHEN IT'S AWAKE.

The Barracuda can be harmful to humans, both outside and inside! Barracuda are a notorious carrier of ciguatera, a kind of fish food poisoning. Ciguatera is the most common type of poisoning from eating fish to affect humans. More than 300 species of fish are suspected of causing ciguatera poisoning, including barracuda, jacks, eels and surgeonfishes. The toxins of ciguatera are believed to start with microorganisms called dinoflagellates, then bigger fish eat them, and the poison goes up the food chain. The poisons are most accumulated and concentrated in the larger fish at the end of the food chain. Ciguatera poison is heat resistant, so cooking does not break it down or eliminate it. The first symptoms of ciguatera poisoning are a tingling around the mouth, tongue, lips and throat. Symptoms can occur a few minutes after eating or as late as 30 hours after consumption of the poisonous meal. It can progress to nausea, muscular weakness and diarrhea. Medical help should be sought because extreme cases can be fatal.

Ciguatera, however, is regional; meaning it is found only in certain places. It is not found in the southern Antilles for instance, but is found around the Bahamas. Barracuda are considered poisonous in Cuba where its sale is prohibited, but it is a favorite food in Puerto Rico.

Captain Spencer Slate of Key Largo, Florida, has trained an 80 pound barracuda named Oscar to eat fish out of his hands, and even right from his mouth.

A dense school of Pacific barracuda, wearing their "hunting stripes," passes over an undersea reef.

35

Can you find the Scorpionfish in this photo?

This scorpionfish has been disturbed, so it flashes the bright spots on its pectoral fins to startle and distract, then it zips away to settle into a new hiding place.

Poisonous Fish

Scorpionfish are masters of camouflage. This one matches the color and texture of the rocks it rests upon, right down to the color of the algae speckled here and there.

Scorpionfish

More than 200 species of fish are protected by venomous spines. Scorpionfish are carnivorous fish that typically rest on the sea bottom or reefs. They have poisonous spines in their fins. Scorpionfish rely on this poison and artful camouflage to protect them. Scorpionfish do a lot of lying around, waiting for a meal to swim their way. They want to go unnoticed by other fish-they don't want their prey to see them, and they don't want bigger, hungry fish to notice them either. The "good-camouflage-plus-poison-spines" strategy must be very successful, because there are lots of different kinds of scorpion fishes found in seas all over the world.

The Spotted scorpionfish is a typical scorpionfish. It is common throughout its range in Florida, the Caribbean, and the Bahamas. It can grow to eighteen inches in length. Like other scorpionfish, it is skillful at matching the color of its background. It has tassel-like flaps of skin all over to match the texture of the rocky reefs and other growths that wave in the current. Sitting very still on the reef, with all these fleshy flaps, waving tassels, and mottled coloring, it is difficult to discover there is a fish there at all!

The Weedy scorpionfish is considered extremely rare, but maybe that is because it is just so hard to find! The Weedy scorpionfish makes its living pretending to be a crinoid. Crinoids are spindly creatures that live on ocean reefs. Small, juvenile fish often hide among the tangled arms of a crinoid, so when a little fish sees the Weedy scorpionfish, thinking it is swimming into a safe place, it swims right into the scorpionfish's mouth.

This Weedy scorpionfish is pretending to be a crinoid, a common coral reef animal. There is a genuine red crinoid just behind the Weedy scorpionfish.

The Decoy fish is a rare species of scorpionfish. It lures prey by raising its dorsal fin, which looks like a small fish-complete with imitation eye and mouth! Attracted by the lure, the victim investigates and is eaten.

If you should be punctured by a scorpionfish's venomous spines, you will find the sting painful but probably not fatal. Try immersing the affected area in water that is as hot as you can stand. The hot temperature of the water will destroy the venom. The pain can last for hours, but usually it will decrease if treated immediately with heat. After you destroy the toxin with heat, you must also take care that you do not get an infection from an unclean wound. Fishes' spines are covered with bacteria and other marine growth, so cleaning any wound is important.

The Spiny Devilfish

The Spiny devilfish, a kind of scorpionfish, is a triple threat. It usually hides in the sandy sea bottom, almost totally covered up with just its camouflaged eyes and upturned mouth exposed. It is waiting to gulp up unsuspecting passersby. It also has the poisonous spines that scorpionfish are famous for, and it has a third trick, a special startle-and-disappear again escape plan.

If the Spiny devilfish is caught walking around exposed on the sea floor, it can suddenly spread out its fins and make a startling display of flashy color and patterns. The tail and pectoral fins are usually folded up next to the fish's sides, and the bright parts can not be seen. The fish makes a sudden flash of color in the face of a predator, then quickly folds its fins back against its body and settles into the sea floor some distance away. Hopefully its camouflage coloring will make it disappear again from sight.

The Spiny devilfish can sometimes be seen walking slowly along the sandy sea bottom with what looks like long, bony fingers. The "fingers" are actually specially modified rays of its pectoral fins. The devilfish can use these special "hands" to turn over rocks while searching for food.

This Spiny devilfish was caught out walking around on the sandy seafloor, so it makes a big display of the flashy colors on its fins and tail. While the attacker is surprised, the devilfish quickly darts away.

The devilfish has bony "fingers," which it uses to walk along the seafloor. It can even turn over stones with its long, thin fingers.

The sneaky devilfish spends a lot of time hidden in the sand, with just its eyes and pouty mouth sticking out, waiting for fish to swim by.

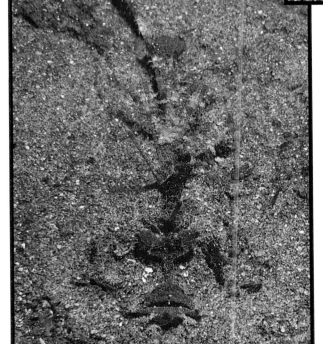

The Moses sole, found in the Gulf of Aqaba near the Sinai Peninsula, secretes a poison that can paralyze a shark!

Blue Meanies

This Twinspot lionfish, or Two-eyed lionfish, has "fake" eyes on its tail, which can confuse prey long enough for the lionfish to eat them, or make predators hesitate long enough to escape.

With all the lionfish's flaps, tassels and stripes, it might take a little fish too long to figure out which end of the lionfish has the mouth!

When a small fish realizes too late that it has been surrounded by the lionfish's big fins, it tries to escape between the rays of the fins—only to be caught in the lionfish's transparent fin-connecting skin.

Lionfish

Lionfish are a subfamily of scorpionfishes. They have greatly enlarged pectoral fins, and elongated dorsal fin spines. These have the effect that when a lionfish slowly drifts over the reef, it has a stately and extravagant appearance-but the sly lionfish is actually using its wide fins to sweep wide areas of water to gather up little fish for a meal.

Some of the thin skin between the rays of the fins is not colored, but is transparent. When a small prey fish realizes it is in a dangerous trap, it will make a last-minute dash for safety-but in its panic, it might dash straight into the transparent skin, instead of escaping out the gaps between the rays of the fin. The lionfish is then able to pull the captured fish up to its mouth by neatly curling up its agile fins.

Lionfish have cryptic eye coloration to help disguise where its eye might be. Cryptic coloration refers to colors that help hide or disguise an animal. Lionfish have many stripes all over their body, and the stripe through their eye looks like all the others. The stripe helps hide the round shape of the eye. The large projections over the eyes, and the irregular flaps of skin hanging from the mouth, also are probably distracting and confusing to prey the lionfish is hunting. When the lionfish is drifting ever so slowly toward its prey, it hopes the targeted fish won't realize which end has its eyes, and its mouth!

Stonefishes

Stonefishes carry the most potent venom of all fishes. Beneath their warty skin are 12 to 14 spines, each with its own large venom sack attached to the base. Their neurotoxin (a poison that affects nerves) can be fatal to humans in just a few minutes. More of the same poisonous spines are also on the stonefish's fins. The tough, grooved spines can easily penetrate a tennis shoe, and people are often injured when they accidentally step on a stonefish while wading in shallow sea-water. The stonefish is equally dangerous when found on a beach, because they can live out of water up to ten hours! *Synanceja horrida,* a type of stonefish, has the largest venom glands of any known fish, and a victim poisoned by this fish can die in intense agony within six hours.

Victims of stonefish stings do not always die, but the wound is always extremely painful and can result in the death of surrounding tissue, and the loss of punctured fingers or toes. The stonefish is fairly common on sandy flats and shallow lagoons in Micronesia. Its excellent camouflage and its habit of burying itself in the sand make it nearly invisible.

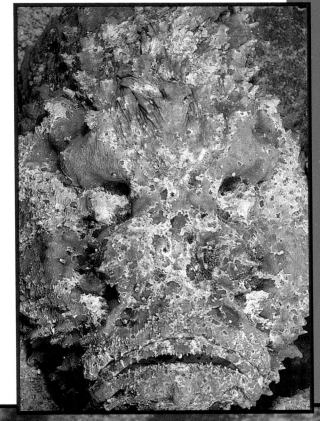

The stonefish is not known for its good looks, and its incredible colors, shapes and textures usually make it difficult to see the ugly fish at all. The neurotoxin found in stonefishes spines affects human nervous systems, and can be lethal.

The stingbull fish has poisonous stings in its fins and gills—yet fishermen consider it an excellent eating fish.

Blue Meanies

The saltwater striped catfish looks cute, but it has poisonous spines on its dorsal and pectoral fins.

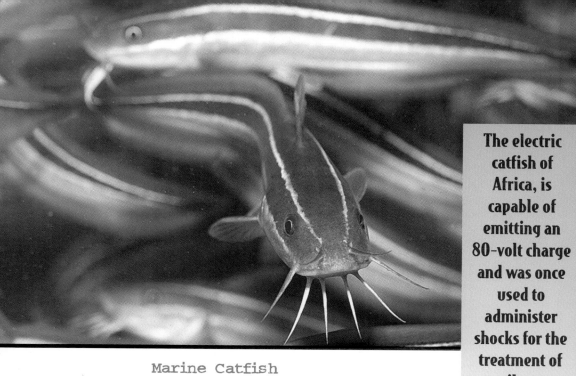

Marine Catfish

Most of the world's 2,000 species of catfishes live in fresh water. Only two families of catfish occur in marine waters, and only the Striped Eel Catfish is likely to be encountered on a reef. It has a single highly venomous spine at the beginning of its first dorsal fin, and on each of its pectoral fins. Wounds from these spines can be dangerous, and even fatal in rare cases.

The skeleton of a species of saltwater catfish found in the West Indies looks like Jesus on the cross, and was actually used by early missionaries in place of wooden or metal crucifixes.

Pufferfish

Pufferfishes are named for their ability to greatly inflate themselves by drawing water or air into a specialized chamber near their stomachs. While underwater there is no air to "inhale," so puffer fish swallow water in order to distend their bodies for protection. If a puffer fish, however, is brought out of the sea into the air, it is able to gulp air and "puff up" too!

Puffers are able to increase up to three times their normal size. In this state, the tough little fish becomes as hard as a football. They do this maneuver to discourage other fish from swallowing them as a meal. Also, it is a nifty way to wedge themselves in holes and cracks in the reef to prevent being dragged out by a predator.

Puffers have one of nature's most powerful poisons, called tetraodotoxin. This poison can be found in their guts, their reproductive organs, and their skin. Some puffers can emit poison through their skin in mucus. Sometimes aquarium owners are surprised to find all of the fish in their tank suddenly dead, except the pufferfish. What happened was that the puffer felt stressed and secreted its mucus. If the concentration of poison in the water gets too high, it will kill the puffer too!

The teeth of puffers are fused into a beak-like structure. They use these hard plates to crunch up coral reefs, and sift out bits of food to eat. By crushing up coral they contribute to making fine sand on the ocean bottom.

Most pufferfish species have the same general shape, and they can be difficult to tell apart. This is further complicated by the fact that most puffer fish are also able to dramatically change their color.

Some pufferfish have no olfactory (smelling) organs and apparently rely heavily on their vision. Puffers typically have large, protruding eyes.

Some species of pufferfish have spines that lie flat against their bodies when the fish is calm, but when the fish becomes alarmed and inflates, the spines stand up and the fish suddenly looks like a prickly ball. These kinds of puffer fish are appropriately called Porcupine fish. The Porcupine fish is an unpleasant spiky punishment to the mouth of any creature that tries to eat it.

Puffer fish can change their shape dramatically. Normally they look pretty much like a typical fish, but when the puffer is alarmed, it gulps up water and inflates into a hard-to-swallow round ball.

Normally a porcupine fish swims around with its spines laying flat against its skin, but when frightened, its spines stick out like hundreds of sharp needles.

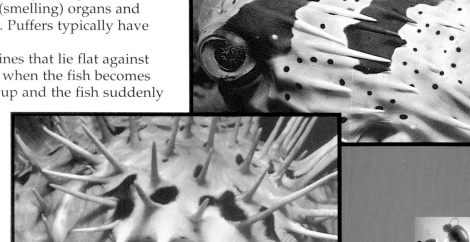

41

Blue Meanies

Considered a delicacy in Japan, fugu are often adored in a religious ceremony prior to be eaten.

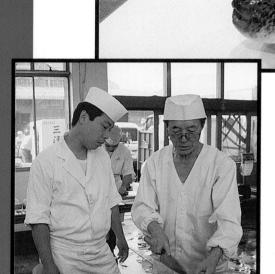

Cooks in Japan who want to serve fugu must train for three years and pass special tests to assure the safety of their future diners.

Fugu

Fugu is a tropical saltwater puffer fish that contains a powerful natural poison that is the number one cause of fatal food poisoning in Japan-yet it is a popular food delicacy. In English, we call this notorious fish "the death puffer" or maki-maki. This special pufferfish lives in a broad stretch of ocean from the Red Sea across the Indian Ocean, and much of the South Pacific. The fugu pufferfish is so poisonous it is sometimes eaten in Japan as a means of committing suicide.

Within the fugu, its viscera (guts) and its reproductive organs contain the powerful alkaloid poison tetraodotoxin. This virulent poison can kill anyone who eats even a moderate amount—less than one-tenth of a gram can kill an adult in as little as 20 minutes. Sufferers of tetraodotoxin poisoning may remain conscious but cannot swallow, see, speak or move. Cooks in Japan who prepare fugu are required to train for three years and must take licensing exams. Restaurants that choose to serve the risky dish also have to be licensed.

Fugu pufferfish are one of the highest priced food fishes in Japan! Wealthy Japanese pay handsomely to eat this risky food. The cook preparing the fugu tries to retain just enough of the toxin to produce a numbing sensation on the lips and tongue of the diner. Some diners apparently like the thrill of flirting with death, but there are about fifty deaths a year from too much "thrill" being left in poorly prepared fugu!

In Japan puffer fish are inflated, then dried, and made into garden lanterns.

Bad tempered and fearless, a disturbed Sarcastic fringehead will attack anything— even divers.

Sarcastic Fringehead Fish

This large and grouchy member of the blenny family lives on the sea bottom off California's coast. Fringeheads can grow up to one foot in length, and are found in shallow water.

Male fringeheads are especially remarkable, having an enormous mouth that extends the full length of the head, back to the very edge of his gill covers. Cranky males use their big, flared mouths to attack and wrestle with neighbors.

When fringeheads choose a home on the sea bottom, it might be an abandoned burrow or empty seashell. They like to be grumpy homebodies and hardly ever leave their comfy spot, except to grab something to eat, or to scare off an intruder. Their bad tempers make them almost fearless, and Sarcastic fringeheads are known to even attack scuba divers that unwittingly swim too close.

When on the attack, the Sarcastic fringehead flares open his special mouth quite wide, showing a bright yellow edge, and rows of jagged, sharp teeth. If the target of the attack is another nasty fringehead, the confrontation escalates into a mouth-wrestling competition. Usually the fish with the biggest mouth wins. The victorious grouch stays at his location, and the loser leaves to find a different neighborhood.

Despite their aggressiveness, Sarcastic fringeheads make surprisingly tender and careful fathers. The male Sarcastic fringehead protects his clutch of fertilized eggs by holding them in his mouth. This unusual behavior is called mouth brooding.

THE **LAFF** found in the Indian Ocean **IS THE MOST POISONOUS OF ALL FISH** – IT BURROWS INTO THE SAND, AND STEPPING ON THE HOLLOW SPINES OF ITS BACK BRINGS PAINFUL DEATH

The male Sarcastic fringehead threatens his neighbor by flaring his large wide mouth in a display of ferocity. Fringeheads typically only leave their shell homes to threaten other fish or human divers.

43

This is a genuine cleaner goby. Notice how much the sneaky saber-toothed blenny below resembles this real cleaner fish.

Just Plain Nasty

Saber-Toothed Blenny

Many fish in the ocean enjoy a special relationship with certain smaller fish—a cleaning service. The larger fish is cleaned of parasites and dead skin by accommodating littler fish. The "cleaner fish" benefit by getting a free meal—and it receives some protection by having the larger fish so near.

A deceitful trickster, however, has learned to take advantage of this well-known cleaning routine.

The saber-toothed blenny has a wicked, hooked mouth on the underside of its head, armed with two nasty fangs for digging a bite out of unsuspecting fish.

The saber-toothed blenny is a small fish that looks just like a common cleaner fish. The evil saber-toothed blenny does the same swimming dance that genuine cleaner fish do to attract a client fish. However, when the bigger fish approaches for a cleaning, the treacherous blenny makes its move. The saber-toothed blenny quickly takes a bite out of the unsuspecting fish, then makes a fast dash for a safe hole in the reef. The larger fish is left stunned and bleeding.

Real cleaner fish have tiny, comb-like teeth to carefully groom their host fish, but a saber-toothed blenny has a pair of wicked teeth hidden in its lower jaw. This sneaky fish has even been known to nip at the legs of skin divers.

After the saber-toothed blenny has made its hit-and-run attack, it hurries back to its safe hole in the reef.

Yellowtail Tangs

Yellowtail tangs are gentle herbivores that graze on algae found on sun-dappled rocks in shallow areas. They look totally harmless as they move over reefs in small, loose schools.

Yellowtail tangs, however, have a special defense to use against predators. It requires the attacker to be quite close, so this defense is used only as a last resort. At the slender curve in their bodies where the tail begins, there are three protruding spines. These spines are very sharp, and are used to make a last moment slash against any threat. The effectiveness of these spines in creating deep gashes in other fish has earned them their other common name—Yellowtail Surgeonfish.

Some surgeonfish have spines that work like switchblades. In these species, the spine is folded down into a groove, most of the time, but when the fish feels threatened, the spines are erected to "operate" on anything that comes near.

Yellowtail tangs also have a kind of defensive camouflage: a vertical line that runs through their eyes. The idea is that a rushing predator might not clearly see the tang's eye, and so not have time to figure out which way the tang will swim off.

Yellowtail tangs look harmless enough, but really they are always ready for a fight, and can be quite aggressive.

This close up photo of the curved part of the tang, where the fish's body meets its tail, reveals three spines in a row. Tangs use these sharp blade-like spines as a last minute defense against attackers— earning them the nickname "surgeonfish."

The hatchling surgeonfish hardly resembles its parents at all, and is often mistaken for other species.

Tangs have lines running through their eyes to disguise their faces. If a predator aims at the back end of the tang, mistaking the dots there for the fish's eyes, it will receive a cutting slash from the protective spines.

Here's a close up you never want to witness in person: the razor sharp fangs of a hungry piranha!

ANGLER TOM WHITAKER of Brampton, Ont., Canada, CAUGHT A RED-BELLIED PIRANHA IN A RESIDENTIAL LAKE NEAR HIS HOME!

The knifelike teeth of piranhas are used by natives in South America as arrow tips.

Piranhas

To the Indians of the Amazon basin, the word piranha means "fish tooth." Many natives use the jaws of piranhas as cutting tools and the common household name for scissors is also "piranha!"

Piranha are divided into two subfamilies, one carnivorous, and one herbivorous. *Serrasalminae* are the carnivores, there are 20 different species of these fierce little meat eaters. *Mylinae* are the herbivores, of which there are more than 50 different species. The fruit-eating piranha can grow quite large, up to 44 pounds. These herbivorous piranhas, also called pacu, have a second row of teeth in each jaw. The meat-eating piranhas only have one row of teeth in each jaw.

The fierce meat-eaters prefer quiet pools and slow sections of streams and rivers. For the most part they eat fish. They become a danger to humans if they become stranded in isolated pools, which may happen during a drought, and are starving. In this case they become fearless and will attack any intruder, regardless of size. It is reported that the combination of razor-sharp teeth and powerful jaw muscles allows piranhas to snap off a man's toe or finger like a carrot. Piranha quickly gather whenever anything out of the ordinary takes place, and will attack with lightening speed any creature making a commotion in the water. Even a wounded crocodile was reportedly stripped of all its flesh in less than five minutes.

A researcher traveling through South America in 1963 reported that although he did not hear about a single death due to piranha, he did find that most of the adult native population had lost fingers, toes or penny-sized chunks out of their arms or legs after bathing in the local rivers.

To thwart thieves, jewelers in Sweden exhibit valuable rings in aquariums filled with flesh eating piranhas.

On September 19, 1981, more than 300 people were killed and eaten by piranha when an overloaded passenger-cargo boat capsized and sank as it was docking at the Brazilian port of Obidos.

46

Eels

Scientists say that eels are long fishes that: lack pelvic fins, have continuous upper and lower fins that connect with a pointed tail, have no scales (or almost no scales), have no gill rakers, and have reduced or skimpy skeletons. There are 730 species of fish that match this description, including moray eels and conger eels.

When baby eels are just hatched they can gather in such a tight tangle that they look like a wound ball of yarn.

The glass eel of Australia is so transparent that the pages of a book can be read through its body.

Eels can swim backward, and if they are placed on wet grass, they can create enough friction pushing off the ground to slowly "swim" out of water.

An eel in the Zoological Station at Rovigno, Italy that had lost its upper jaw in an accident lived without eating for four years!

In 1992, Trevor Kerrison caught a giant eel off the coast of Plymouth, England that weighted 111.5 pounds and was 7 feet 11 inches in length.

A close up look at a spotted garden eel coming out of its hiding place in the sand.

THE SHIP THAT HAD A LEAK PLUGGED UP BY AN EEL!
The S.S. ALCOA PIONEER, TAKING ON WATER IN ITS HOLD, LIMPED INTO DRYDOCK AT MOBILE, ALABAMA, WHERE IT WAS DISCOVERED THAT A HOLE IN THE BOTTOM OF THE SHIP HAD BEEN EFFECTIVELY PLUGGED BY AN EEL!

The conger eel can swallow and digest metal fishhooks.

Blue Meanies

This is a gold-spotted snake eel. Notice the long tubes extending from its nostrils. Eels are known for having weak eyesight, but an excellent sense of smell.

The blue and yellow ribbon eel has extravagant nostril extensions that help the eel "scoop up" promising smells in the water.

A group of garden eels extend from their burrows to nip at passing nourishment in the current. These tiny, slender eels are notoriously shy and difficult to approach.

Blue Meanies

The electric eel cannot live out of water—yet it can be drowned by holding it under water.

This Hawaiian Conger eel uses its nostril tubes to sniff the water. It rests in its reef hole during the day, and hunts at night using its acute sense of smell.

In New Zealand a popular pastime for swimmers is to float on innertubes through underground cave rivers that are filled with eels.

Muraena hellina, a type of moray eel considered a food delicacy by the ancient Romans, were fed rebellious slaves.

The Mustache Conger eel of Hawaii is nocturnal; meaning it is most active at night. Being a nighttime predator, it is likely to rely more on smell than vision to find food. Most fish have only nostril pits or holes in their faces (called nares), but the Conger eel has well defined tubular nostrils. This is a good indication of how important their sense of smell is. Conger eels grow more than 4 feet in length, and are considered a food delicacy in Hawaii.

On May 31st, 1948 Japan celebrated a Memorial Day for the souls of 25,000,000 eels eaten by the Japanese in 1947!

Eels in the Anatoki River, near Takahe, New Zealand, are so tame they will eat from a spoon.

"Friends, Romans, Countrymen, Lend Me your Ears."

Roman politician Marcus Crassus (115 – 53 BC) had a pet eel that wore a jeweled necklace and earrings.

Roman Emperor Claudius' mother had pet eels that wore pearl earrings.

Hortensious (114 – 50 BC), a Roman orator and attorney, wore mourning for a full year after the death of his pet eel. Apparently ancient Romans were desperate for pets. The real mystery, however, is how were the earrings attached to the eels, since eels have no ears?

LUCIUS CRASSUS (140-91 B.C.) ROMAN LEGAL LUMINARY WAS SO FOND OF HIS TRAINED LAMPREY THAT HE GAVE IT EARRINGS AND A PEARL NECKLACE AND WHEN THE FISH DIED *HE WORE MOURNING FOR AN ENTIRE YEAR*

Lampreys

Lampreys belong to the primitive group of fish called Agnatha that branched off from the ancestors of modern fish before the evolution of jaws. Even so, they do have one very advanced sense: a kind of "electric radar." Sea lampreys maintain an electric field around their heads, which enables them to sense objects in the dark. If the field is "deformed" they know that another object has entered the range of their "radar"—and can attack it.

Sea lampreys are fearless in attacking larger fish. Once a sea lamprey has attached itself to a victim, it won't let go. It continues to rasp away at the victim's body and suck its blood and fluids until the victim finally dies. Even great whales, especially Sei whales, are found with oval scars caused by lampreys. Perhaps the breaching (leaping) behavior of whales is an attempt to dislodge parasitic lampreys?

Lamprey eels move from the sea to freshwater to breed. There they construct large nests which maybe three feet high and 4 feet in diameter. Both parents labor together using the powerful suction of their mouths to move rocks that can weigh twice their own weight. The Latin genus name *Lampetra* actually means "stone sucker." Females may produce tens of thousands of eggs in a single spawn.

Lampreys have done great damage to the fishing industries in North America's Great Lakes. They first entered the Great Lakes through the Erie Canal in 1825. In 1929 they were able to come through the Welland Canal to reach the upper Great Lakes. When the St. Lawrence Seaway system was completed in 1959, it allowed the lamprey access to the entire Great Lakes. Today, the lamprey is still only barely kept under control by annually poisoning the shallow areas where eel larvae are found.

Hagfish

Marine hagfishes are found throughout the world. They are jawless scavengers with degenerate (useless) eyes. Hagfish feed by boring into dying and dead creatures, often consuming them from the inside out. The hagfish fastens itself to the gills of large fishes from where it works its way into the inside of the body. It then devours all the flesh without breaking the host's skin. Hagfish produce extraordinary amounts of slime that can be used for defense by clogging the gills of predatory fishes. When feeding, hagfish tie their bodies into knots to gain extra leverage for tearing off flesh. They also contort their bodies to wipe their own slime off themselves. Tanned hagfish skin is the primary source of "eel skin" leather used in wallets, purses, and other fashionable accessories.

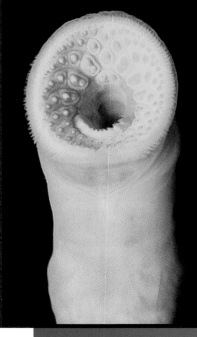

Blue Meanies

A lamprey's circular mouth has such great sucking power that they can lift rocks twice their own weight. The sharp teeth near the center of the mouth cut the victim's skin, and the lamprey feeds on its life juices until the victim is dead.

(left) A close up look at the slime producing pores of a hagfish. The slime is used as a defense mechanism and enables the hagfish to attack prey much larger than itself. (right) Once completely covered under its canopy of mucus, few fish will dare attack it fearing suffocation brought on by clogged gills.

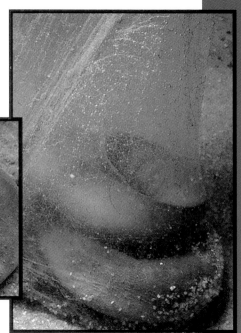

A deep water creature, the hagfish rests on the ocean floor until food comes along, then attaches itself to its prey by entering through the victim's gills.

49

Blue Meanies

The spotted moray has poor eyesight and hunts mainly at night , by smelling its prey.

Moray eels need to continuously open their mouths in order to breathe. This exposes their many teeth and gives them a very frightening appearance.

Looking much like a dead leaf, this strange transparent creature is the larvae of a deep sea eel.

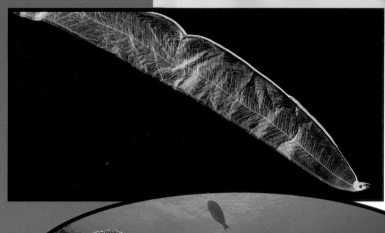

Morays are usually very cautious about swimming freely in the open ocean exposed to predators.

That's a Moray

Moray eels are true eels. They have no scales, and no pectoral fins. Morays are a very successful type of fish, with probably hundreds of different species found worldwide. Like most eels, morays undergo a lengthy larval stage wherein the tiny young eels are pelagic (drift in the wide-open ocean).

Most morays are more active at night, when they like to come out to hunt. Morays have poor sight and hunt mostly by smell. Many fishes sleep at night, nestled in cracks in reefs. Morays try to "sniff out" these sleeping fishes. The shape of a moray's teeth gives a clue as to its choice of food. Eels with long, sharp canine teeth eat fishes and octopus, those with rounded or conical teeth tend to eat crustaceans like crabs or lobsters.

Morays are edible and are hunted for food throughout much of the world. Large eels in the tropics, however, often have ciguatuera poison and so should not be eaten.

Although morays are fish, they do not have the same gill covers that most fish have; instead they have a small opening on the side of their heads. Morays must continuously open and close their mouths to pump oxygen and water over their gills. This gives them a fierce appearance, because when they gape continuously, they expose their impressive teeth.

Eel Look-a-Likes

Wolf eels look a little like wolves with their grey coloring, and large protruding teeth. They, like wolves, leave their dens at night to go on the hunt. Wolf eels of course, aren't wolves. Wolf eels may look like eels, with long bodies topped by a continuous dorsal fin, but they are not really eels. True eels do not have pelvic fins.

Wolf eels can grow up to 8 feet long, and are impressive to see when they leave their rocky dens to swim. When they stop to rest, Wolf eels can prop themselves up with their pectoral fins to survey the situation around them.

Wolf eels like cold, dark water. Around the Pacific coast of Canada they can be found in shallow waters. Around the coast of Southern California they are found down deeper, perhaps in 100 feet of water, because they have to go deeper to find the cold temperatures they like. Wolf eels are typically found in crevices between rocks or in dark spaces on old shipwrecks.

The wolf eel has a grumpy look to its face, but it is often found with a loving mate. It is a sight to see two big, toothy Wolf eels squeezed into the same narrow crevice, both trying to look out into the sea at the same time. Apparently mating for life, the fond couple shares the same hole in a reef. After the female lays a large egg mass inside their den, both fish stay to guard their prize.

Sometimes scuba divers will feed Wolf eels one of their favorite foods-the prickly sea urchin. Divers break the urchin open with a knife or rock, and the "eel" smells the treat and comes out of its den to eat it. It is possible to "train" these "eels" in this way, so Wolf eels familiar with divers will often leave their dens and swim toward a diver as soon as they see one. This can be intimidating if the diver approaching is not aware of the routine.

The closely related "wolf fish," found on the East Coast of Canada, reaches a maximum length of 7 feet. They have very strong jaws and can easily crush a fully-grown lobster or crab or the largest of whelk shells. They have a reputation for being cranky and stubborn, and are liable to bite onto whatever is near and not let go—including boat railings and paddles!

Propped up like a cobra ready to pounce, the wolf eel has a very strong bite that can puncture metal.

It is fairly easy to train wolf eels to come out of their rocky homes for a free hand-out, in this case a tasty sea urchin.

THE **PELICAN EEL**
WHICH HAS BEEN FOUND AT DEPTHS OF 3,000 FEET,
CAN STRETCH ITS MOUTH AND GULLET
TO SWALLOW FISH LARGER THAN ITSELF

Sea Monsters: REAL & *Imaginary*

Through the centuries many people claim to have seen a "sea monster" in Scotland's Loch Ness. Scientists have been unable to find hard physical evidence of the monster, but still the legend continues.

The Loch Ness Monster

The most famous sea monster in the world is Nessie, the Loch Ness Monster. Nessie, as it is fondly called, is believed by some people to inhabit Scotland's Loch Ness, a long deep fresh water lake. The first reported sighting was in the sixth century. St. Columba, a Scottish holy man, witnessed a beast threatening a swimmer in the lake. The holy man made the sign of the cross and shouted out, "Think not to go further, touch not that man!" Amazingly the beast retreated, swimming backward more rapidly than it had been swimming forward. Through the ages many other "sea monsters" have been discovered to be rare and interesting fish.

Loch Ness,
Scotland

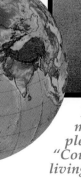

Believers think that Nessie and other reported "sea monsters" might actually be prehistoric creatures called plesiosaurs. In this painting by Sir Peter Scott, entitled "Courtship in Loch Ness," Scott imagines a pair of "Nessies" living in the dark murky depths of the lake.

Oarfish

The scientific name for the oarfish is *Regalecus glesne*, which means King of the herring! The Japanese call it "the king of the palace under the sea."

Oarfish average 20 – 30 feet in length, but are rarely seen alive. Occasionally one will wash up on a beach somewhere, and it creates a commotion when people find it. On September 19, 1996, a group of U.S. Navy Seals found a 22-foot long, 300 lb. oarfish washed up on the beach in Coronado, California. The oarfish's size and snake-like shape encourage ideas of sea serpents.

The Oarfish has a tall red "comb" of spines on its head, and a bright red dorsal fin that runs the whole length of its body. Its long, red pelvic extensions rotate like the oars of a rowboat when it swims, thus its common name. Scientists, however, think the long appendages may actually be used in taste perception rather than as a swimming aid. If we assume that an oarfish sometimes swims at the surface, and might poke its head out of the water, we can guess that people might describe it as a sea serpent.

In 1848, an English ship named Daedalus was sailing near the Cape of Good Hope and the whole crew saw:

> ". . . an enormous serpent, with head and shoulders kept about four feet constantly above the surface of the sea and as nearly as we could approximate by comparing with the length of what our main topsail yard would show in the water, there was at the very least 60 feet of the animal . . . it had no fins, but something like the mane of a horse, or rather a bunch of seaweed, washed about its back."

This description came from Peter M'Quhae, the captain of the Daedalus, who was responding angrily to a request from the English Admiralty that he confirm or deny the rumors about a sea serpent. For the creature that the sailors saw to have been 60' long, it might be guessed that it was one female oarfish being followed by two interested males.

Even though it is big enough and flashy enough, the oarfish doesn't really make a good sea serpent. It doesn't have any teeth and is so slender it is almost transparent. It actually has a fragile look, out of the water, and scientists consider it totally harmless to humans.

In Japan, the deep-sea oarfish helps scientists predict earthquakes by swimming to the surface from depths of over 200 meters.

This is a rarely seen baby oarfish. Its distinctive head and lond slender shape are in evidence, but the bright red coloring of the fins associated with this fish, have not yet developed.

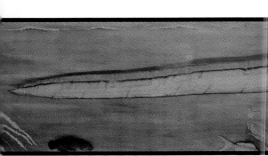

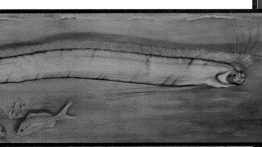

The oarfish which grows to a length of 40 feet and is responsible for many tales of fearsome sea serpents can't even bite—because it has no teeth.

Sea Monsters

Guitarfish do not have scales and their tough skin lends itself to the cutting, twisting and drying necessary in "monster making." The monster created from the carcass is actually viewed from the bottom side of the guitarfish.

This is a finished Diable de mer, custom made sea monster. The eyes of the monster are actually the nostril openings located on the underside of the fish's head.

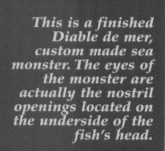

Diable de Mer

There is one "sea monster" which is known worldwide by many different names. The French call it Diable de Mer, "Devil of the Sea." In 1554 a professor of medicine at Montpellier called it De pisce Episcopi habitu, "The fish dressed as a bishop." An illustration by Ulysses Aldrovandi in 1613 called it a "SeaEagle" and Monstrosi piscus volantis imago, "the image of a monstrous flying fish!" In 1928 an Australian ichthyologist said he could not account for the common name of the creature being Jenny Haniver, and wondered if it might have been a fisherman's wife.

Actually, it is a guitarfish! You can make one into a sea monster yourself. First you need to catch a guitarfish. Cut the fins so they look like wings, and put the supporting cartilage of the fins into a position you like. These will protrude and look like arms. Tie string around the area where the neck should be. Stretch the nostril openings (on the bottom side of the fish) to make sure they look like eyes. The gaping mouth will stick out more and more as the skin dries and shrinks. You can twist the tail around to whatever position you like. If the fish is a male, it will have twin claspers that you can position to look like hind legs. After it is well dried, you can coat it with varnish to protect it. Voila! You have your own sea monster.

The Coelacanth—A Prehistoric Sea Monster

Fossils of the coelacanth fish have been found dating to 75 million years ago. This strange fish was believed extinct until a living specimen was captured in 1938 off South Africa. The first coelacanth created a huge sensation when it was brought to the world's attention. It was very exciting news and ignited imaginations to think perhaps prehistoric sea monsters and "extinct" fish could live in the sea and go unnoticed.

Popularly called the Tasselfoot when it was first discovered, the coelacanth has four fins with bones and joints that are suggestive of primitive legs. Some scientists believe that ancestors of this rare fish may have crawled onto land and been the ancestors of all vertebrates, including humans.

A second coelacanth was not found until 1952, but there have now been more than 170 coelacanths collected since its "rediscovery," and scientists believe there is an estimated 370 to 500 individual specimens living off the west coast of the Comoro Islands in the Indian Ocean. Coelacanths normally live in deep water, and usually die when brought up to the surface. Coelacanths have been observed by scientists in submersibles swimming along the ocean bottom at a depth of six hundred feet. From these observations it is now known that coelacanths are active at night and during the day sleep in groups in lava caves. The contents of their stomachs reveal that they eat squid and reef fish.

Coelacanths are now protected by the Comoro government and it is illegal for fishermen to sell them to anyone other than the government. There is a rumor among some Far Eastern people that the oily fluid found in the coelacanth acts as a life-prolonging potion. This could prove dangerous for the coelacanth, in the same way that rumors that rhinoceros' horn has special medicinal qualities has led to the illegal hunting of rhinos by poachers.

Rarely seen in their natural habitat, coelacanths are black with large white splotches that camouflage them in their lava cave homes off the Comoro Islands.

Studying dissected dead coelacanths, scientists have discoverred that the nostril openings on the top of the fish's head do not connect to the mouth cavity, suggesting that they are totally non-functional.

Coelacanths are serious predators! Observers in submersibles report that they sneak up on their prey, and make a sudden lunge with their mouths wide open (much like groupers), propelled by their large powerful tails.

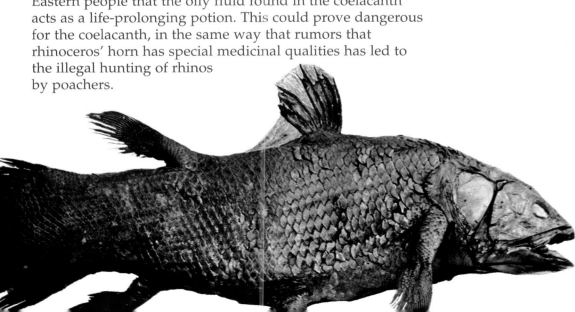

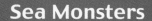

Half woman, half fish, mermaids depicted in art are usually voluptuous and beautiful.

Not exactly "beautiful," it is hard to imagine how sailors mistook the gentle manatee of the tropics for mermaids of myth.

Christopher Columbus in 1492 noted in his journal the sighting of three mermaids. In all likelihood what his sailors actually saw were Caribbean manatees, a slow moving gentle sea mammal.

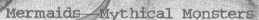

Mermaids—Mythical Monsters

The myth of a creature that is half human, half fish can be traced as far back as 5000 BC, to the Sumerian-Babylonian fishtailed god Oannes. The Babylonians believed that Oannes left the sea at daytime and returned to it at night, which would account for the god's amphibious appearance.

Christopher Columbus, on January 9, 1493 during a voyage to the New World, wrote in his captain's log that one of his seamen sighted three sirens, or mermaids, but that they were "not as beautiful" as artists portrayed them. What the sailor probably saw were manatees, a large lazy sea mammal with a paddle-like tail.

It is ironic that the manatee is probably the source for the mermaid myth. These marine mammals do resemble humans in that they breathe air, and the females have mammary glands between their forelimbs (fore-flippers). One has to wonder, however, what the lonely sailors were thinking of when they described manatees as being voluptuous, beautiful sirens trying to tempt them too close to the rocks!

In 1620, Captain Sir Richard Whitbourne sailed to Newfoundland to investigate the possibilities of English settlements. He reported seeing a mermaid who he described as being quite beautiful, but instead of hair it had "many blue streaks." It approached the boat, but one of Sir Richard's sailors clobbered it with an oar, and it sank beneath the sea.

P. T. Barnum's "Feejee" Mermaid

In 1842, Phineas Taylor Barnum was told about a Boston sea captain who had bought a preserved mermaid while on a voyage to Calcutta in 1817. The captain tried exhibiting it for a while in Europe to recover the $6,000 he paid for it, but then he died, and left the strange treasure to his son. The son sold it to the proprietor of the Boston Museum. Although the museum proprietor did not put it on exhibit, he did contact P.T. Barnum, the famous sideshow entrepreneur.

Instead of quickly putting the mermaid on exhibit, Barnum decided to manufacture some excitement.

An anonymous letter appeared in an Alabama newspaper saying:

Dr. Griffin, agent of the Lyceum of Natural History in London . . . had in his possession a most remarkable curiosity, being nothing less than a veritable mermaid taken among the Feejee Islands, and preserved in China, where the Doctor had bought it for a high figure . . .

More of these kinds of letters appeared in different newspapers, and a New York newspaper published a story with a Washington dateline, by an anonymous correspondent, who hoped "the editors of the Empire City would beg a sight of the extraordinary curiosity before Dr. Griffin took ship for England." Indeed Dr. Griffin (actually an accomplice of Barnum named Levi Lyman) did allow newspaper editors to peek at his mermaid, and they obligingly wrote supportive articles about its authenticity.

P.T. Barnum then complained publicly that Dr. Griffin would not sell him his mermaid to exhibit. Meanwhile, Barnum had woodcut illustrations made and ready for use in advertisements. The newspapers faithfully reported all this and used the conveniently supplied woodcut illustrations, too. Barnum soon announced that he had managed to arrange to show this mermaid for "positively one week only!" at a concert hall on Broadway—complete with educational discussion by Dr. Griffin.

Eventually the much-promoted mermaid was moved across the street to Barnum's museum. The mermaid display was a great success, and pulled in thousands of dollars a week.

Barnum was so proud of himself that in later years he told the entire story of his carefully orchestrated publicity. In his autobiography, he described the Feejee Mermaid as an "ugly, dried-up, black-looking specimen about three feet long . . . that looked like it had died in great agony."

It is now commonly known that the mermaid trophies, which were so popular in the 1800s, were manufactured in Japan and Asia, using skeletons of monkeys joined to taxidermied fishes. For this revelation we can thank one Robert Ripley who acquired one of these legendary "mermaids" and displayed it at his New York City Odditorium in 1939, revealing the taxidermy hoax and exposing the myth of the "Feejee Mermaid" forever.

Believe It or Not!

P. T. Barnum hired an artist to etch this woodcut illustration of his "veritable mermaid." The illustration helped create the public demand to see Barnum's mermaid, and in turn made a fortune for the wily entrepreneur.

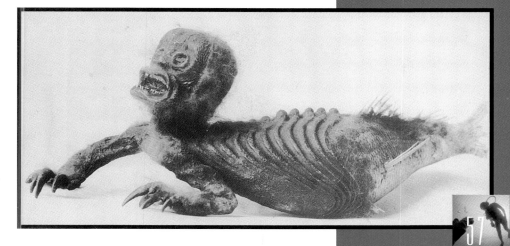

Acquired by Robert Ripley in the Orient in 1932, this "Feejee Mermaid" is part monkey, part fish, cleverly sewn together by an Asian taxidermist.

Agmathids– The group of jawless fishes that includes lampreys and hagfishes.

Amphibious– An animal that can live on both land and in the water.

Anonymous– Where the name of a person is not known or acknowledged.

Appendages– An external organ or body part.

Bioluminescence– "Cold" (without producing any heat) light generated by living organisms.

Carnivorous– An animal that eats flesh.

Caviar– An expensive salty food prepared from the eggs of sturgeon and certain other fish.

Chondrichthyes– The group of cartilaginous fishes that includes sharks, skates and rays, that have a cartilage skeleton rather than a bony skeleton.

Ciguatera– Food poisoning caused by toxins found in some large fish.

Crinoids– Also known as "feather stars" and "sea lilies;" primitive organisms with feathery arms that are related to starfishes.

Cryptic coloration– Colors or patterns that help camouflage an organism.

Dinoflagellates– Tiny, usually one-celled planktonic organisms. Some can produce toxins poisonous to fishes that eat them.

Estuaries– River mouths that have been flooded by the ocean.

Exothermic– Reactions in which there is a release of heat.

Ichthyologist– An expert or specialist in the branch of zoology dealing with fishes.

Luminescent– Exhibiting "cold" light.

Millisecond– One one-thousandth of a second.

Mucus– A thick slimy secretion produced for protection.

Muscular contraction– A shortening of muscle fibers.

Nares– Small holes, similar to nostrils, in a fish, used for smelling.

Neurotoxin– A poison that affects the nervous system.

Nocturnal– Referring to a creature that is most active at night.

Olfactory– Referring to the sense of smell.

Osteichthyes– The largest group of modern fishes; all members have a bony skeleton.

Pelagic– Referring to the open sea, generally away from the shore, reefs, or bottom.

Phosphorescent– Giving off light, without noticeable heat or combustion.

Photopore– A bioluminescent organ, generally shaped like a tiny pocket with a transparent cover that allows light to shine out.

Plankton– Organisms that drift at the mercy of ocean waves and currents.

Protrusion– A thing that is thrust-out, or juts out.

Scutes– Enlarged and hardened plate-like scales like those found in rows along the body of sturgeons.

Sequential hermaphroditism– The natural process whereby an organism changes from one sex to another as it matures.

Spawning– The production of eggs and milt by organisms for reproduction.

Submersible– A container, or ship, that can be immersed in water, especially one that holds people, cameras, or equipment, for underwater studies.

Symmetrical– When the parts of something match in size, shape and position.

Tetraodotoxin– A very powerful poison produced in the viscera and reproductive organs of pufferfishes.

Thermal inertia– The maintenance of a constant body temperature due to having a large massive body that cools very slowly.

Underslung jaw– Where a creature's lower jaw does not project as far forward as its upper jaw.

Venomous– Poisonous, relating to the ability to inject poisons.

Viscera– The internal organs of a body, especially the abdomen. Guts.

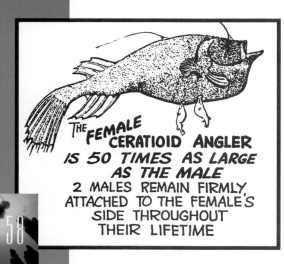

THE **FEMALE** CERATIOID ANGLER IS 50 TIMES AS LARGE AS THE MALE 2 MALES REMAIN FIRMLY ATTACHED TO THE FEMALE'S SIDE THROUGHOUT THEIR LIFETIME

The Chinese fish of Australia, is edible 9 months of every year, but is poisonous during June, July and August.

Sarcastic fringehead

Index

59

Photo Credits

t=top
tl=top left
tr=top right
tm=top middle
m=middle
ml=middle left
mr=middle right
b=bottom
bl=bottom left
br= bottom right